孫子 SUN TZU'S 兵法
THE ART OF WAR
—————— A GRAPHIC NOVEL ——————

ILLUSTRATIONS BY PETE KATZ

San Diego, California

Canterbury Classics
An imprint of Printers Row Publishing Group
9717 Pacific Heights Blvd, San Diego, CA 92121
www.canterburyclassicsbooks.com • mail@canterburyclassicsbooks.com

Canterbury Classics
Publisher: Peter Norton
Associate Publisher: Ana Parker
Acquisitions Editor: Kathryn C. Dalby
Editorial Team: JoAnn Padgett, Melinda Allman, Dan Mansfield

Quid Publishing
Publisher: Mark Searle
Associate Publisher: Emma Bastow
Creative Director: James Evans
Managing Editor: Isheeta Mustafi
Senior Editor: Lucy York
Designer: Lyndsey Harwood
Illustrator and script writer: Pete Katz

Conceived, designed and produced by The Bright Press, an imprint of The Quarto Group.
1 Triptych Place, London, SE1 9SH, United Kingdom.
(0)20 7700 6700 • www.quarto.com

Library of Congress Cataloging-in-Publication Data

Names: Sunzi, active 6th century B.C., author.
Title: The art of war: a graphic novel / Sun Tzu.
Other titles: Sunzi bing fa. English
Description: San Diego, CA : Canterbury Classics, 2018.
Identifiers: LCCN 2017060553 (print) | LCCN 2018004521 (ebook) | ISBN 9781684125043 | ISBN 9781684124299 (thread-bound)
Subjects: LCSH: Military art and science--Early works to 1800--Comic books, strips, etc. | Graphic novels.
Classification: LCC U101 (ebook) | LCC U101 .S94913 2018 (print) | DDC 355.02--dc23
LC record available at https://lccn.loc.gov/2017060553

Printed in China

27 26 25 24 23 5 6 7 8 9

CONTENTS

INTRODUCTION

The Art of War is undoubtedly the most famous handbook for military strategy ever written. It was first published in the 5th century BC and was written by Sun Tzu, a military general who lived during the Eastern Zhou period of Chinese history (779-471 BC). There is a huge amount of mythos surrounding him, perhaps the most notorious story being how he impressed Ho Lu, the king of Wu, with his effectiveness and earnestness by decapitating two of Ho Lu's favorite concubines during a demonstration of his theories. We must bear in mind, though, that historical tales inevitably get embellished over time, intertwining fact and myth.

Indeed, sometime around AD 1101-1200 academics started to believe that Sun Tzu never actually existed at all, as there was no mention of him in historical records from that period. And in the early days of the Chinese republic, a Chinese writer and reformer, Liang Qichao, speculated that the book might have been written instead by Sun Tzu's descendant Sun Bin around the 4th century BC. This theory was backed by several mentions of a military treatise written by Sun Bin from that period.

But in 1972, bamboo slip writings called the Yinqueshan Han slips were discovered in tombs that had been sealed since the Han dynasty (206 BC-AD 220). Among the slips were two separate military texts, one credited to Sun Tzu and the other to Sun Bin. The content in both texts overlapped a great deal and it became clear that Sun Tzu's text was the earlier and Sun Bin's work was an expansion of the previous text. This at last explained the historical confusion, as various historical accounts had been mentioning one of two Master Suns who had both written a treatise on war.

Despite the age of the work, the fascination with *The Art of War* has remained constant and it continues to have a presence in bookstores today. It is on the recommended reading list for all U.S. military intelligence personnel. The more widespread appeal of Sun's work is that it can be applied to many fields beyond that of military battle, most commonly in the business arena, where the lessons can be adapted to corporate strategy and office politics. It is common reading for business executives and people at management level, and is also utilized by lawyers for trial strategy, and by sports managers and coaches who apply the theories to game preparation and psychology.

The book is available in many languages and was first translated into English in 1910 by Lionel Giles. When you compare English translations, it is interesting to see that the earlier versions are much more concerned with faithfully translating the language of Sun, almost word for word, sometimes to the detriment of the overall meaning. More recent translations have been less concerned with the exact language Sun used in favor of the real essence of his teachings.

This book is based primarily on the Lionel Giles text, though I have also drawn inspiration from some of the more modern translations. It is not trying in any way to be the best interpretation of *The Art of War*. Just an alternative, perhaps an illustrated addition to a fan of Sun Tzu or a colorful introduction to this ancient text that has stood the test of time and remains relevant today.

CHINA. SOMETIME DURING THE HAN DYNASTY*.
A BOY, STILL HALF ASLEEP, MAKES HIS WAY TO A SECLUDED BUILDING FOR ANOTHER DAY'S LESSONS...

* HAN DYNASTY: 206 BC-AD 220

GOOD MORNING, SIFU.

AH! GOOD MORNING, LIU! COME, HAVE SOME TEA. I'M SURE THE CLIMB WAS TIRING.

THANK YOU, SIFU. A DRINK BEFORE TRAINING WOULD BE NICE.

NO TRAINING TODAY. JUST THEORY. IT'S ABOUT TIME WE STARTED ON SUN TZU'S TEACHINGS.

THAT OLD THING? I WAS HOPING TO CONTINUE SWORD TRAINING THIS WEEK.

THE KNOWLEDGE YOU WILL LEARN FROM SUN TZU WILL AID YOU FAR MORE THAN THE SHARPEST OF SWORDS, MY BOY.

I CAN SEE YOU'RE NOT CONVINCED. BUT IN TIME, YOU'LL AGREE WITH ME. NOW DRINK YOUR TEA AND LISTEN.

PART ONE

MAKING PLANS

SUN TZU SAID: *WAR IS A HEAVY UNDERTAKING. IT IS A PLACE OF LIFE AND DEATH. A ROAD TO EITHER SAFETY OR DESTRUCTION.*

THEREFORE, IT MUST BE MEDITATED ON MOST CAREFULLY.

THE ART OF WAR IS GOVERNED BY FIVE FUNDAMENTALS, TO BE FACTORED INTO ONE'S DELIBERATIONS, WHEN SEEKING TO ASSESS ALL SITUATIONS IN AND OUT OF BATTLE.

THESE ARE: THE WAY, WHICH UNITES MEN IN AIM WITH THEIR RULERS, FOLLOWING THEM EVEN TO DEATH.

HEAVEN, WHICH SIGNIFIES NATURE. NIGHT AND DAY, THE WEATHER, TIME, AND SEASONS.

EARTH, WHICH ENCOMPASSES DISTANCE BOTH SHORT AND LONG, HEIGHT AND DEPTH, DANGER AND SAFETY, OPEN OR NARROW SPACES, AND LASTLY, LIFE AND DEATH.

COMMAND, WHICH MUST INVOLVE WISDOM, SINCERITY, COMPASSION, COURAGE, AND STRICTNESS.

DISCIPLINE, WHICH IS THE STRUCTURE OF THE ARMY, THE COMMAND CHAIN, AND MILITARY EXPENDITURE AND LOGISTICS.

EVERY COMMANDER WILL BE FAMILIAR WITH THESE FIVE FUNDAMENTALS.

UNDERSTAND THEM AND SUCCEED, MISAPPREHEND THEM AND FAIL.

WHEN SEEKING TO ASSESS THE CONDITIONS OF A SITUATION, YOU MUST DETERMINE:

WHICH LEADER BENEFITS FROM THE WAY?

WHICH OF THE TWO GENERALS IS MOST ABLE?

WHICH SIDE HAS THE ADVANTAGES OF HEAVEN AND EARTH?

WHICH SIDE IS MORE DISCIPLINED?

WHICH ARMY IS BOTH MORALLY AND PHYSICALLY STRONGER?

WHICH SIDE HAS BETTER TRAINED OFFICERS AND MEN?

IN WHICH ARMY IS REWARD AND PUNISHMENT MOST FAIR AND CONSTANT?

ANSWERING THESE SEVEN QUESTIONS WILL ENABLE US TO FORESEE VICTORY OR DEFEAT.

THE GENERAL WHO HEEDS THESE WORDS WILL CONQUER. MAY HIS COMMAND BE LONG! THE GENERAL WHO IGNORES THESE WORDS WILL ONLY SUFFER DEFEAT. LET HIM BE AT ONCE DISMISSED!

USE THESE RULES TO YOUR BENEFIT WHEN MAKING PLANS BUT ALSO AVAIL YOURSELF OF ANY HELPFUL CIRCUMSTANCES. IF CONDITIONS CHANGE AND BECOME MORE FAVORABLE, THEN MODIFY YOUR PLANS ACCORDINGLY.

ALL WARFARE IS BASED ON DECEPTION.

WHEN STRONG AND ABLE, APPEAR WEAK.

WHEN UTILIZING YOUR FORCES, APPEAR INACTIVE.

WHEN NEAR, APPEAR FAR AWAY.

WHEN FAR AWAY, APPEAR CLOSE BY.

TEMPT YOUR ENEMY WITH BAITS.

MIMIC DISORDER, THEN DESTROY HIM.

IF YOUR ENEMY IS SECURE, JUST PREPARE FOR HIM.

IF HE IS STRONGER, EVADE HIM.

IF HE IS QUICK TO ANGER, IRRITATE HIM. PRETEND TO BE WEAK, SO THAT HE GROWS ARROGANT.

IF HE IS RESTING, HARASS HIM.

IF HIS FORCES ARE UNITED, DIVIDE THEM. ATTACK WHEN HE IS UNPREPARED, APPEAR WHERE YOU ARE NEVER EXPECTED.

YOUR PLANS THAT ENCOMPASS THESE STRATEGIES MUST NOT BE DIVULGED BEFOREHAND.

THE GENERAL WHO WINS A BATTLE HAS MADE MANY CALCULATIONS BEFORE THE BATTLE IS EVEN FOUGHT.

THE GENERAL WHO LOSES HAS SPENT LITTLE TIME MAKING CALCULATIONS BEFOREHAND.

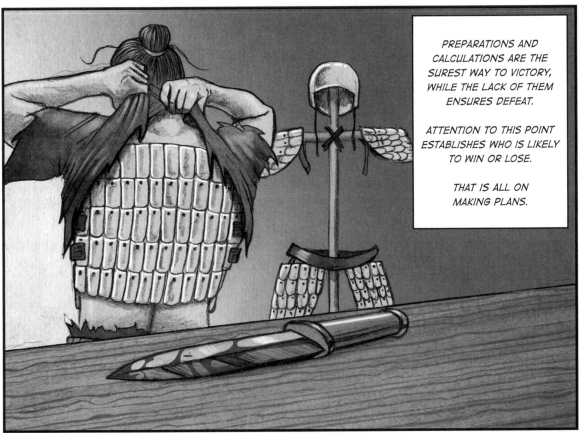

PREPARATIONS AND CALCULATIONS ARE THE SUREST WAY TO VICTORY, WHILE THE LACK OF THEM ENSURES DEFEAT.

ATTENTION TO THIS POINT ESTABLISHES WHO IS LIKELY TO WIN OR LOSE.

THAT IS ALL ON MAKING PLANS.

AND THAT IS THE FIRST PART COMPLETED. HOW DID YOU FIND IT?

MORE INTERESTING THAN I THOUGHT I WOULD, SIFU. PARTICULARLY THE PART ABOUT DECEPTION.

AND YOUR THOUGHTS ON THAT PART?

A CLEVER GENERAL PLAYS WITH HIS ENEMY LIKE YOUR CAT PLAYS WITH A MOUSE. PRETEND WEAKNESS OR LAZINESS...

...THEN SUDDENLY POUNCE UPON HIM.

VERY GOOD, YOUNG MASTER. I'M GLAD SOME OF IT AT LEAST HAS SUNK IN.

IT DOESN'T SEEM VERY HONORABLE, THOUGH. WOULDN'T A FIGHT BETWEEN TWO EQUALLY STRONG SIDES BE A FAIRER WAY TO WIN A BATTLE?

NO ONE EVER ENTERS WAR WITH FAIRNESS IN MIND. ARMIES STRIKE WHEN THEY FEEL THEY HAVE THE ADVANTAGE. AN EQUALLY MATCHED BATTLE WOULD BE LONG, WITH MANY DEATHS.

I SUPPOSE...

IF YOU COULD END A WAR SWIFTLY, WITH FEW CASUALTIES, EVEN UNFAIRLY, WOULDN'T YOU DO IT?

YOU'RE PONDERING. THIS IS GOOD. YOU HAVE MADE YOUR FIRST STEPS IN UNDERSTANDING THE ART OF WAR. WE'VE MADE AN EXCELLENT START.

I THINK NOW WOULD BE A PERFECT TIME FOR SOME FRESH TEA.

IN NO TIME...

ARE YOU READY FOR THE SECOND PART, MASTER LIU?

I AM, SIFU.

GOOD. THE SECOND PART IS CALLED WAGING WAR.

DON'T GET TOO EXCITED, THOUGH. THIS PART PROBABLY ISN'T WHAT YOU IMAGINE.

IT IS PRIMARILY CONCERNED WITH THE PRICE OF WAR. "HE WHO WISHES TO FIGHT MUST FIRST COUNT THE COST."

PART TWO

WAGING WAR

SUN TZU SAID: *IN WAR, CONSIDER AN ARMY IN THE FIELD CONSISTING OF ONE HUNDRED THOUSAND ARMORED SOLDIERS. ADD TO THIS ONE THOUSAND SWIFT CHARIOTS, ANOTHER THOUSAND HEAVILY ARMORED WAGONS, AND ENOUGH PROVISIONS FOR ALL THE MEN AND HORSES FOR FOUR HUNDRED MILES.*

YOU WILL ALSO HAVE MANY COSTS AT HOME AND AT THE FRONT, INCLUDING BRIBES AND ENTERTAINMENTS OF GUESTS AND ENVOYS, SMALL ITEMS LIKE GLUE AND PAINT, AND REPAIRS TO ARMOR AND CHARIOTS.

THE COST OF ALL THIS, FOR RAISING AN ARMY OF ONE HUNDRED THOUSAND MEN, EASILY REACHES ONE THOUSAND OUNCES OF SILVER **PER DAY***.*

IN WAR, VICTORY SHOULD BE QUICK. IF VICTORY IS SLOW, THEN MEN'S WEAPONS WILL GROW DULL, THEY WILL TIRE, AND THEIR MORALE WILL DROP. LAYING SIEGE TO A TOWN WILL EXHAUST YOUR STRENGTH.

A LONG CAMPAIGN PUTS A STRAIN ON THE RESOURCES OF THE STATE.

IF YOUR MEN ARE TIRED, WITH DULLED SWORDS, LOW MORALE, AND NO MORE FUNDS, OTHER RULERS WILL TAKE ADVANTAGE OF THIS AND ATTACK.

THEN THE WISEST OF MEN WOULD BE UNABLE TO AVERT THE ENSUING CONSEQUENCES.

WE HEAR THAT HASTE TO WAR IS STUPID, BUT DELAY IS EQUALLY UNWISE. NO COUNTRY HAS EVER BENEFITED FROM A LENGTHY WAR.

SIFU, I DO NOT UNDERSTAND. WHICH IS BETTER, THEN— HASTE OR CAUTION?

ESSENTIALLY SUN TZU HINTS THAT WHILE SPEED IS SOMETIMES RASH, TARDINESS CAN NEVER BE ANYTHING BUT FOOLISH...

...IF ONLY BECAUSE IT MEANS POVERTY TO THE NATION.

IT IS ONE OF THE MANY QUESTIONS THAT YOU WILL ONLY BE ABLE TO PROPERLY ANSWER WHEN YOU ARE FACED WITH THE PROBLEM YOURSELF.

ONLY ONE WHO KNOWS THE DISASTROUS EFFECTS OF A LONG WAR CAN REALIZE THE SUPREME IMPORTANCE OF RAPIDLY BRINGING IT TO A CLOSE.

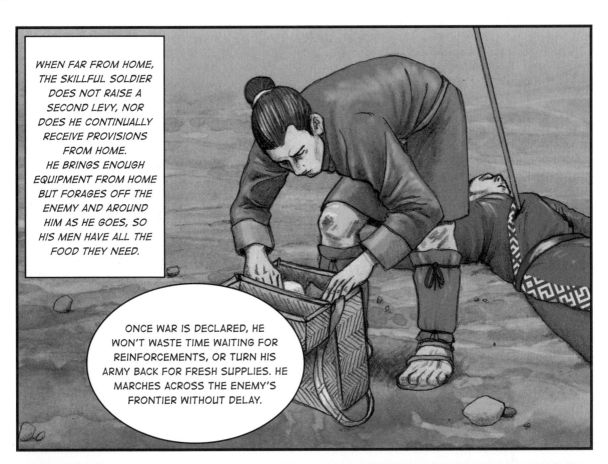

WHEN FAR FROM HOME, THE SKILLFUL SOLDIER DOES NOT RAISE A SECOND LEVY, NOR DOES HE CONTINUALLY RECEIVE PROVISIONS FROM HOME.
HE BRINGS ENOUGH EQUIPMENT FROM HOME BUT FORAGES OFF THE ENEMY AND AROUND HIM AS HE GOES, SO HIS MEN HAVE ALL THE FOOD THEY NEED.

ONCE WAR IS DECLARED, HE WON'T WASTE TIME WAITING FOR REINFORCEMENTS, OR TURN HIS ARMY BACK FOR FRESH SUPPLIES. HE MARCHES ACROSS THE ENEMY'S FRONTIER WITHOUT DELAY.

MAINTAINING AND SUPPLYING AN ARMY FAR AWAY DRAINS THE TREASURY AND BRINGS POVERTY TO THE PEOPLE.

AN ARMY IN CLOSE PROXIMITY CAUSES PRICES TO RISE IN PANIC. HIGH PRICES MEAN PEOPLE SPEND MORE, LEAVING THEM LITTLE FOR RENT OR TAXES.

WHILE STRENGTH WEAKENS ON THE BATTLEFIELD, FAMILIES AT HOME ARE POVERTY-STRICKEN. THE PEOPLE LOSE SEVEN-TENTHS OF THEIR INCOME.

BROKEN CHARIOTS, WORN-OUT HORSES, ARMOR AND HELMETS, BOWS AND ARROWS, SPEARS AND SHIELDS, OXEN AND WAGONS COST THE TREASURY SIX-TENTHS ITS TOTAL REVENUE.

HENCE A WISE GENERAL SEES THE IMPORTANCE OF FORAGING OFF THE ENEMY.
ONE CARTLOAD OF THE ENEMY'S PROVISIONS IS WORTH TWENTY BROUGHT FROM HOME. A SINGLE OUNCE OF ENEMY FEED IS WORTH TWENTY FROM ONE'S OWN STORES.

BECAUSE TWENTY CARTLOADS WILL BE CONSUMED IN BRINGING ONE CARTLOAD TO THE FRONT LINES.

TO KILL THE ENEMY, AROUSE YOUR MEN TO ANGER. REWARD THEM WITH THE SPOILS SO THEY SEE THE ADVANTAGES OF SUCCESS.

IN CHARIOT FIGHTING, FOR INSTANCE, WHEN TEN OR MORE ENEMY CHARIOTS HAVE BEEN TAKEN, REWARD THE MAN WHO TOOK THE FIRST. CHANGE THE ENEMY FLAGS AND MINGLE THE CHARIOTS WITH YOUR OWN. THE CAPTURED SOLDIERS SHOULD BE TREATED WITH KINDNESS AND RESPECT. USE YOUR VANQUISHED FOE TO BOLSTER YOUR STRENGTH.

IN WAR, LET YOUR OBJECT BE SWIFT VICTORY, NOT AN EPIC CAMPAIGN.

A GREAT GENERAL, UNDERSTANDING OF WAR, IS THE ARBITER OF THE PEOPLE'S FATE. IT FALLS TO HIM WHETHER THE NATION FACES PEACE OR PERIL.

THAT IS ALL ON WAGING WAR.

I HAD NO IDEA HOW MUCH WAR COST. I CAN'T EVEN IMAGINE THAT MUCH MONEY. IT'S A WONDER *ANYBODY* GOES TO WAR.

AND YET THERE WILL ALWAYS BE SOME LORD OR OTHER EAGER TO GO TO WAR, HIS HEAD FULL OF GLORY, WHILE ORDINARY FOLK BEAR THE COST.

≒SIGH≒

WELL, I THINK THAT'S PLENTY TO THINK ABOUT FOR NOW. YOU SHOULD HEAD BACK TO TOWN BEFORE IT GETS LATE.

SEE YOU TOMORROW, LIU.

SEE YOU TOMORROW, SIFU.

PART THREE

STRATEGIC ATTACKS

SUN TZU SAID: IN WAR, IT IS FAR BETTER TO TAKE THE ENEMY'S COUNTRY WHOLE AND INTACT.
SO TOO, IT IS BETTER TO CAPTURE AN ENTIRE ARMY, REGIMENT, DETACHMENT,
OR COMPANY THAN TO DESTROY IT.
HENCE, WINNING EVERY BATTLE IS NOT THE SIGN OF SUPREME EXCELLENCE—BUT DEFEATING
YOUR ENEMY WITHOUT THE NEED TO FIGHT IS.
THE HIGHEST FORM OF WARFARE IS TO ATTACK AND UNDERMINE THE ENEMY'S STRATEGIES FIRST.
THE NEXT BEST IS TO ATTACK AND SUNDER THEIR ALLIANCES.
THEN, NEXT, TO ATTACK THEIR ARMIES.
AND LASTLY, THE WORST AND LAST RESORT IS TO ATTACK AND LAY SIEGE TO A CITY.

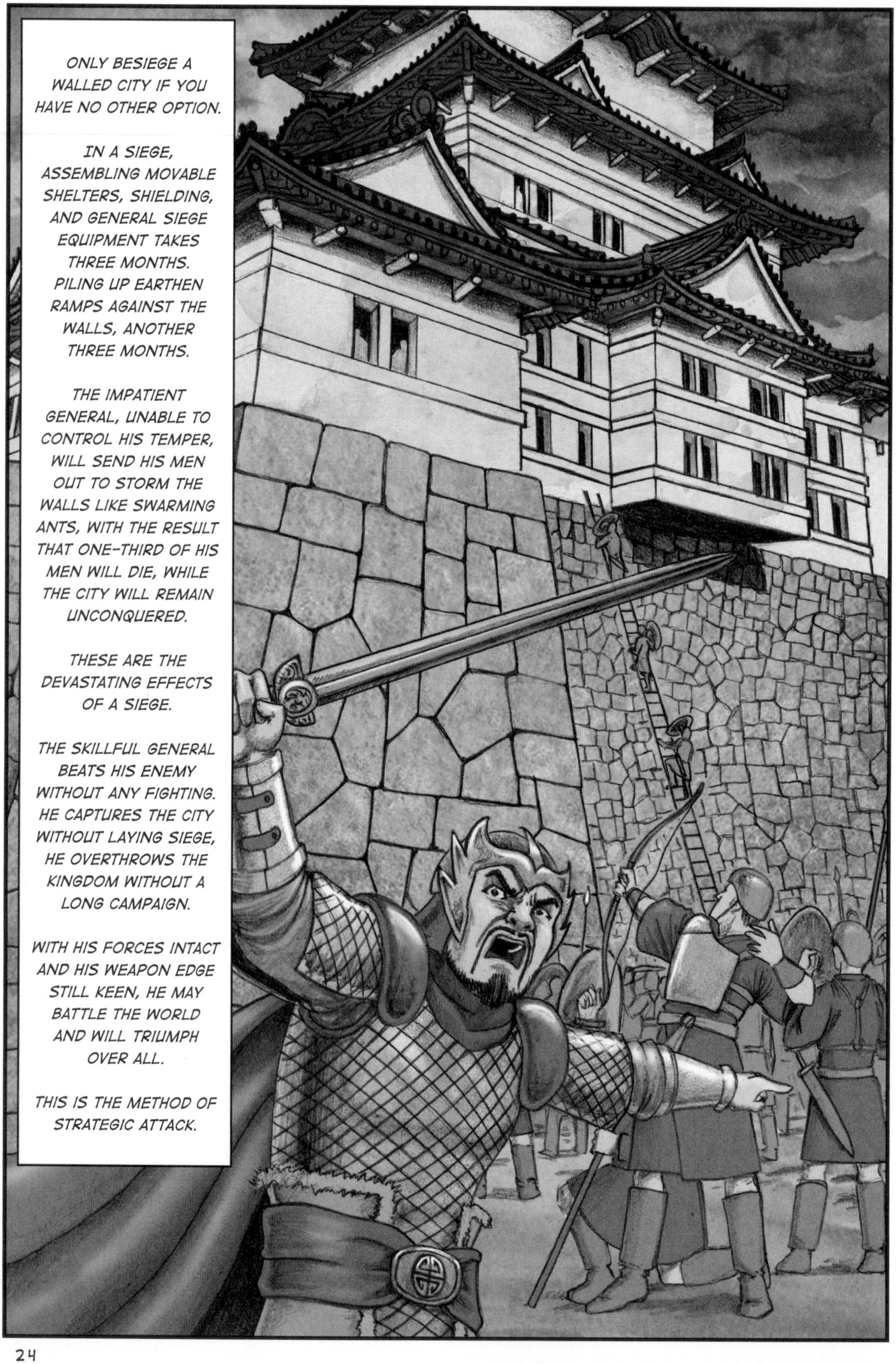
ONLY BESIEGE A WALLED CITY IF YOU HAVE NO OTHER OPTION.
IN A SIEGE, ASSEMBLING MOVABLE SHELTERS, SHIELDING, AND GENERAL SIEGE EQUIPMENT TAKES THREE MONTHS. PILING UP EARTHEN RAMPS AGAINST THE WALLS, ANOTHER THREE MONTHS.
THE IMPATIENT GENERAL, UNABLE TO CONTROL HIS TEMPER, WILL SEND HIS MEN OUT TO STORM THE WALLS LIKE SWARMING ANTS, WITH THE RESULT THAT ONE-THIRD OF HIS MEN WILL DIE, WHILE THE CITY WILL REMAIN UNCONQUERED.
THESE ARE THE DEVASTATING EFFECTS OF A SIEGE.
THE SKILLFUL GENERAL BEATS HIS ENEMY WITHOUT ANY FIGHTING. HE CAPTURES THE CITY WITHOUT LAYING SIEGE, HE OVERTHROWS THE KINGDOM WITHOUT A LONG CAMPAIGN.
WITH HIS FORCES INTACT AND HIS WEAPON EDGE STILL KEEN, HE MAY BATTLE THE WORLD AND WILL TRIUMPH OVER ALL.
THIS IS THE METHOD OF STRATEGIC ATTACK.

IN WAR, IF YOUR FORCES ARE TEN TO THE ENEMY'S ONE, SURROUND HIM; IF FIVE TO ONE, ATTACK HIM, IF TWO TO ONE, DIVIDE YOUR ARMY IN TWO. IF EQUALLY MATCHED, THEN DO BATTLE. IF YOU'RE INFERIOR IN NUMBERS, AVOID THEM. IF FAR WEAKER, THEN FLEE.

MASTER LIU, IF YOU HAD AN ARMY TWICE THE SIZE OF YOUR ENEMY, DO YOU THINK IT WOULD BE A BETTER IDEA TO SPLIT IT IN TWO RATHER THAN MEET YOUR ENEMY IN FORCE?

HMM...SO THAT ONE HALF CAN MEET THE ENEMY HEAD-ON WHILE THE OTHER HALF CAN ATTACK FROM THE SIDE OR REAR... OR FROM ABOVE IF YOU HAD ARCHERS?

INDEED, BOY.

A SMALL FORCE, NO MATTER HOW EFFECTIVE, WILL ALWAYS BE CAPTURED BY A LARGER FORCE.

THE GENERAL IS THE BASTION OF THE STATE. IF THE BASTION IS SECURE, THE STATE IS STRONG; IF THE BASTION IS WEAK, THEN SO IS THE STATE.

THERE ARE THREE WAYS IN WHICH A RULER CAN BRING MISHAP TO HIS ARMY:

BY ORDERING THE ARMY TO ADVANCE OR TO RETREAT AT INCORRECT TIMES. THIS IS CALLED HOBBLING THE ARMY.

BY DISPLAYING IGNORANCE IN MILITARY MATTERS BY TRYING TO GOVERN AN ARMY LIKE A STATE. THIS WILL ONLY CONFUSE AND DISQUIET YOUR MEN.

BY DISPLAYING IGNORANCE IN YOUR ARMY BY EMPLOYING THE WRONG MEN FOR THE WRONG TASKS AND NOT BEING WILLING TO ADAPT. THIS ERODES THE COURAGE OF SOLDIERS.

WHEN AN ARMY IS CONFUSED AND RESENTS ITS LEADER, TROUBLE WILL SURELY COME FROM OTHER RULERS. THE GENERAL HAS BROUGHT CHAOS TO HIS OWN ARMY AND THROWS VICTORY AWAY.

THERE ARE FIVE ESSENTIALS FOR VICTORY:

KNOWING WHEN TO FIGHT, AND WHEN NOT TO FIGHT.

KNOWING HOW TO ORGANIZE LARGE AND SMALL FORCES.

SHARING A COMMON SPIRIT AND WILL WITH YOUR TROOPS.

BEING PREPARED FOR THE UNEXPECTED.

HAVING A CAPABLE GENERAL, UNIMPEDED BY HIS SOVEREIGN.

IF YOU KNOW YOUR ENEMY AND KNOW YOURSELF, IN A HUNDRED BATTLES YOU WILL NEVER BE DEFEATED.

NOT KNOWING YOUR ENEMY BUT KNOWING YOURSELF WILL BRING VICTORY SOME OF THE TIME.

KNOWING NEITHER YOURSELF NOR YOUR ENEMY ENSURES DEFEAT IN EVERY BATTLE.

THAT IS ALL ON STRATEGIC ATTACKS.

FULL KNOWLEDGE OF YOUR ENEMY EQUIPS YOU TO FORM AN EFFECTIVE ATTACK. FULL AWARENESS OF YOUR OWN ARMY ENABLES YOU TO PLAN A POTENT DEFENSE.

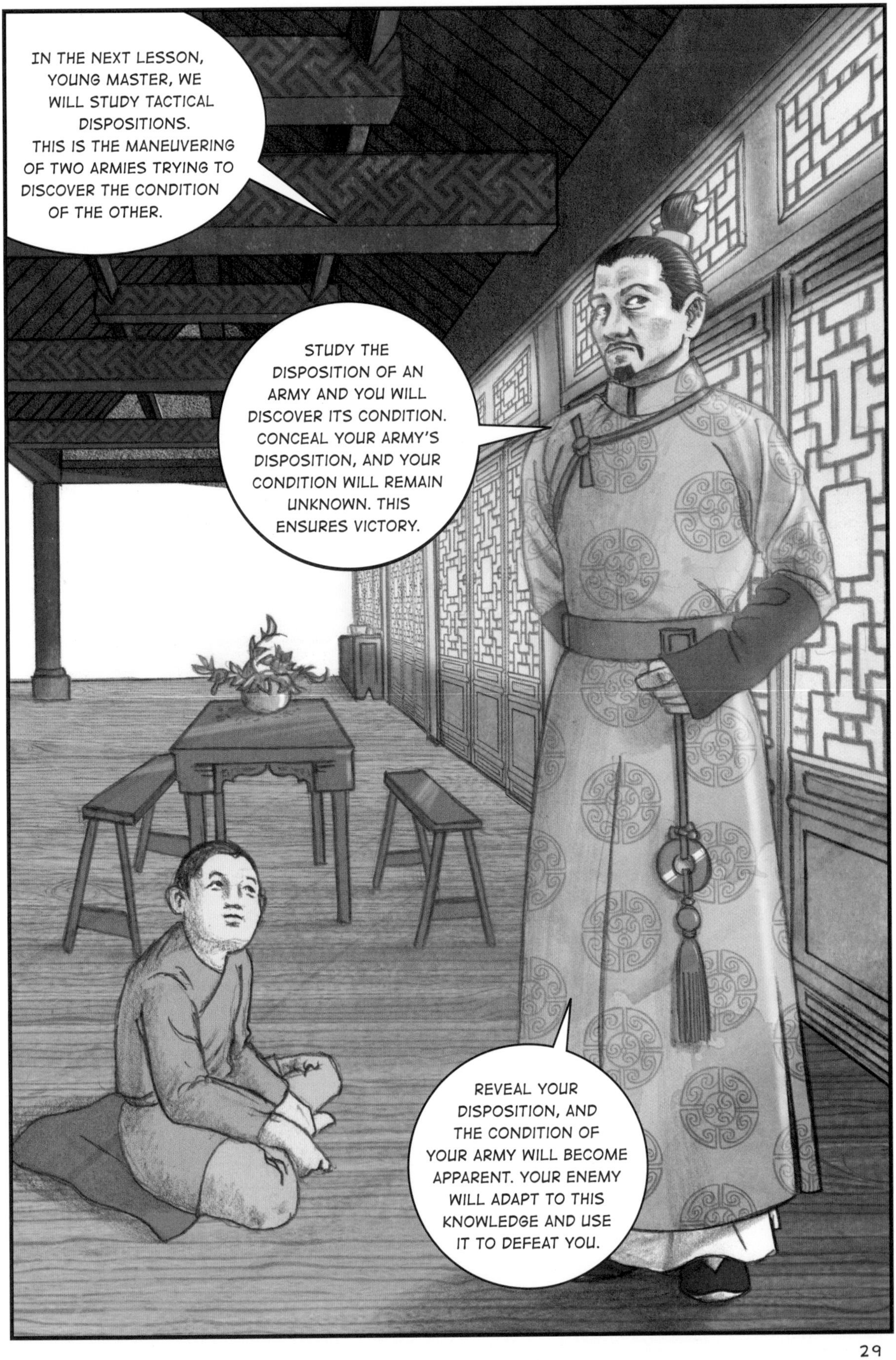
IN THE NEXT LESSON, YOUNG MASTER, WE WILL STUDY TACTICAL DISPOSITIONS. THIS IS THE MANEUVERING OF TWO ARMIES TRYING TO DISCOVER THE CONDITION OF THE OTHER.
STUDY THE DISPOSITION OF AN ARMY AND YOU WILL DISCOVER ITS CONDITION. CONCEAL YOUR ARMY'S DISPOSITION, AND YOUR CONDITION WILL REMAIN UNKNOWN. THIS ENSURES VICTORY.
REVEAL YOUR DISPOSITION, AND THE CONDITION OF YOUR ARMY WILL BECOME APPARENT. YOUR ENEMY WILL ADAPT TO THIS KNOWLEDGE AND USE IT TO DEFEAT YOU.

PART FOUR

TACTICAL DISPOSITIONS

SUN TZU SAID: *THE SUCCESSFUL GENERALS OF OLD FIRST SECURED THEMSELVES FROM WEAKNESS, THEN WAITED TO EXPLOIT WEAKNESS IN THE ENEMY.*

SECURING YOURSELF AGAINST DEFEAT LIES WITH YOU, BUT THE OPPORTUNITY OF DEFEATING YOUR ENEMY IS PROVIDED BY THEM.
THE SKILLED FIGHTER CAN ALWAYS ENSURE HIS INVULNERABILITY, BUT CANNOT ALWAYS BRING ABOUT THE ENEMY'S VULNERABILITY.
HENCE THE SAYING: ONE CAN KNOW HOW TO CONQUER WITHOUT BEING ABLE TO DO IT.

YOU WILL ONLY BE
SECURE AGAINST DEFEAT
WITH GOOD DEFENSIVE
TACTICS. SECURING
DEFEAT OF THE ENEMY
MEANS DELIVERING AN
EFFECTIVE OFFENSIVE.

TAKE A DEFENSIVE
STANCE IF YOUR
STRENGTH IS
INSUFFICIENT;
AGGRESSIVELY ATTACK
WHEN POSSESSING A
SURPLUS OF IT.

THE GENERAL SKILLED IN
DEFENSE HIDES IN THE
MOST SECRET RECESSES
OF THE EARTH.

HE WHO IS SKILLED IN
ATTACK STORMS ACROSS
THE HEAVENS
LIKE LIGHTNING.

THUS, THE GENERAL
ACHIEVES TOTAL
PROTECTION ONE
INSTANT, THEN
COMPLETE VICTORY
THE NEXT.

TO DISCERN VICTORY WHEN EVERY MAN CAN IS NO MARK OF TALENT.
TO BE PRAISED FOR YOUR SKILL AFTER A SUCCESSFUL BATTLE IS NO MARK OF TALENT.
TO SKIN A HARE IN FALL IS NO MARK OF STRENGTH.
TO SEE THE SUN AND MOON IS NO SIGN OF KEEN EYES.
TO HEAR THUNDER, NO SIGN OF SHARP EARS.

CLEVER FIGHTERS WILL NOT ONLY WIN BUT WILL WIN WITH EASE.

THEIR VICTORIES BRING THEM NEITHER FAME FOR WISDOM, NOR PRAISE FOR COURAGE.

THEY ARE SUCCESSFUL BY MAKING NO MISTAKES. ONLY ACTING WHEN VICTORY IS ASSURED.
DOING THIS MEANS CONQUERING AN ARMY ALREADY LOST.

HENCE THE CLEVER FIGHTER ORGANIZES AND ARRANGES HIMSELF WHERE DEFEAT IS IMPOSSIBLE, AND STRIKES AT THE PERFECT MOMENT TO DEFEAT THE ENEMY.

THE STRATEGIC GENERAL ENTERS BATTLE ONLY AFTER THE VICTORY HAS BEEN WON, WHEREAS HE WHO IS DESTINED TO FAIL ENTERS THE FRAY SEARCHING FOR VICTORY THERE.

THE GIFTED LEADER CULTIVATES THE WAY AND ABIDES BY METHOD AND DISCIPLINE; THUS, HE HOLDS VICTORY IN HIS OWN HANDS.

IN WAR, THERE ARE FIVE RULES: MEASUREMENT, ESTIMATION, CALCULATION, COMPARISON, AND VICTORY.

THE GROUND PROVIDES MEASUREMENTS. MEASUREMENT LEADS TO ESTIMATION, WHICH LEADS TO CALCULATION, WHICH FACILITATES COMPARISON, WHICH ALL IN ALL DETERMINES VICTORY.

THUS, COMPARING A VICTORIOUS ARMY TO A DEFEATED ONE IS LIKE WEIGHING A POUND WEIGHT ON A SCALE AGAINST A SINGLE GRAIN.

THE ONRUSH OF A STRATEGICALLY POSITIONED CONQUERING FORCE IS LIKE PENT-UP WATERS BURSTING INTO A DEEP RAVINE.

THAT IS ALL ON TACTICAL DISPOSITIONS.

ON A WARM AFTERNOON IN TOWN...

SO YOU'RE TEACHING THE BOY, THEN?

I AM.

BIT CONCEITED, DON'T YOU THINK? WHAT CAN A USELESS EX-GENERAL LIKE YOU POSSIBLY TEACH HIM?

SUN TZU.

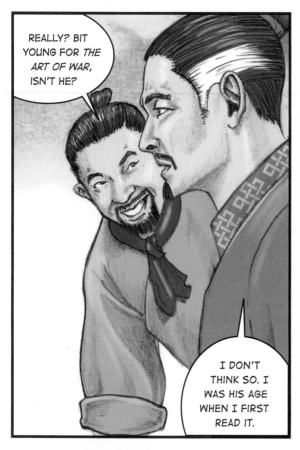

REALLY? BIT YOUNG FOR *THE ART OF WAR*, ISN'T HE?

I DON'T THINK SO. I WAS HIS AGE WHEN I FIRST READ IT.

YES, AND LOOK HOW YOU TURNED OUT!

I THINK I CAME OUT ALL RIGHT. CERTAINLY A BETTER MAN THAN YOU, OLD FRIEND.

OH, YOU THINK SO? SHALL WE TEST THAT THEORY RIGHT HERE AND NOW?

YOU WOULDN'T LAST FIVE SECONDS, WANG. NOW, IF YOUR ARCHERY SKILLS WERE AS SHARP AS YOUR TONGUE, YOU MIGHT ACTUALLY BE DANGEROUS.

PFFT. YOU'RE NO THREAT EITHER. YOU MIGHT SWING A SWORD LIKE A DEMON, BUT YOU WORRY AND FRET LIKE AN OLD LADY.

OH, BE QUIET.

PART FIVE

ENERGY

SUN TZU SAID: CONTROLLING A LARGE ARMY IS THE SAME AS CONTROLLING A SMALL ONE. MERELY DIVIDE THEIR NUMBER INTO REGIMENTS, COMPANIES, AND SO ON. FIGHTING WITH A LARGE ARMY IS THE SAME AS A SMALL ONE. MERELY USING FLAGS AND SIGNALS. WITH DIRECT AND INDIRECT MANEUVERS, YOUR ARMY CAN WITHSTAND THE BRUNT OF AN ENEMY'S ATTACK UNSCATHED. UNDERSTANDING STRENGTH AND WEAKNESS WILL ENSURE MAXIMUM EFFECT FROM YOUR ARMY, LIKE A STONE AGAINST AN EGG.

IN WAR, YOU WILL FIGHT DIRECTLY, BUT WIN INDIRECTLY.

A CLEVER WARRIOR HAS AN INFINITE SUPPLY OF INDIRECT TACTICS AT HIS DISPOSAL. AS INFINITE AS HEAVEN. LIKE THE SUN, MOON, AND SEASONS, THEY END ONLY TO RETURN.

WITH ONLY FIVE MUSICAL NOTES, MORE COMBINATIONS OF MELODIES ARE POSSIBLE THAN CAN EVER BE HEARD.

WITH ONLY THREE PRIMARY COLORS, MORE HUES MAY BE CREATED THAN CAN EVER BE SEEN.

WITH ONLY FIVE BASIC TASTES, MORE FLAVORS MAY BE CREATED THAN CAN EVER BE TASTED.

IN WAR, THERE ARE ONLY TWO METHODS OF ATTACK—DIRECT AND INDIRECT. YET COMBINED, THESE GIVE RISE TO INFINITE POSSIBLE MANEUVERS.

THE DIRECT AND INDIRECT PRECEDE AND FOLLOW FROM EACH OTHER LIKE AN INFINITE CIRCLE.

THE POWER OF RUSHING WATER THAT MOVES BOULDERS IN ITS PATH. THE PRECISION AND TIMING OF A FALCON STRIKING AND DESTROYING ITS VICTIM. YOUR ARMY MUST HAVE BOTH.

A FALCON IS AN EXCELLENT SYMBOL TO USE HERE.

BECAUSE A FALCON DEMONSTRATES NOT ONLY GOOD JUDGMENT IN WHEN THE RIGHT MOMENT TO STRIKE HAS ARRIVED, BUT ALSO THE SELF-RESTRAINT TO HOLD BACK TILL THAT MOMENT.

RESERVE THE FIRE OF YOUR ARMY UNTIL THE VERY INSTANCE IT IS MOST EFFECTIVE.

THE SKILLFUL FIGHTER MATCHES OVERWHELMING POWER WITH PRECISE TIMING.

POWER IS THE BENDING OF A CROSSBOW; PRECISION, THE RELEASE OF THE TRIGGER.

AMID THE TURMOIL OF BATTLE, ALL MAY SEEM CHAOS TO YOUR ENEMY AND YOUR TROOPS IN COMPLETE DISORDER, BUT STILL VICTORY IS ASSURED.

YOUR SIMULATED DISORDER IS BUILT ON DISCIPLINE, FEAR BUILT ON COURAGE, WEAKNESS ON STRENGTH.

HIDING ORDER BENEATH THE CLOAK OF DISORDER REQUIRES CAREFUL DIVISION.

CONCEALING COURAGE UNDER FALSE TIMIDITY REQUIRES A STORE OF LATENT ENERGY.

MASKING STRENGTH WITH WEAKNESS RELIES ON TROOP DISPOSITION.

THE GENERAL SKILLED AT ROUSING THE ENEMY MAINTAINS FALSE APPEARANCES, ENSURING THEY FOLLOW.
HE OFFERS BAIT TO ENTICE THE ENEMY.
THEN, WITH A BODY OF HANDPICKED MEN, HE LIES IN WAIT.

THE GOOD GENERAL LOOKS TO THE EFFECT OF COMBINED ENERGY, AND DOES NOT REQUIRE TOO MUCH FROM INDIVIDUALS.

HENCE HIS ABILITY TO PICK OUT THE RIGHT MEN AND UTILIZE COMBINED ENERGY.

SO, THE GENERAL CONSIDERS THE POWER OF HIS ARMY AS A WHOLE, THEN ASSESSES THE TALENTS OF HIS INDIVIDUAL SOLDIERS AND PLACES THEM IN THEIR MOST EFFECTIVE POSITIONS?

INDEED, YOUNG MASTER.

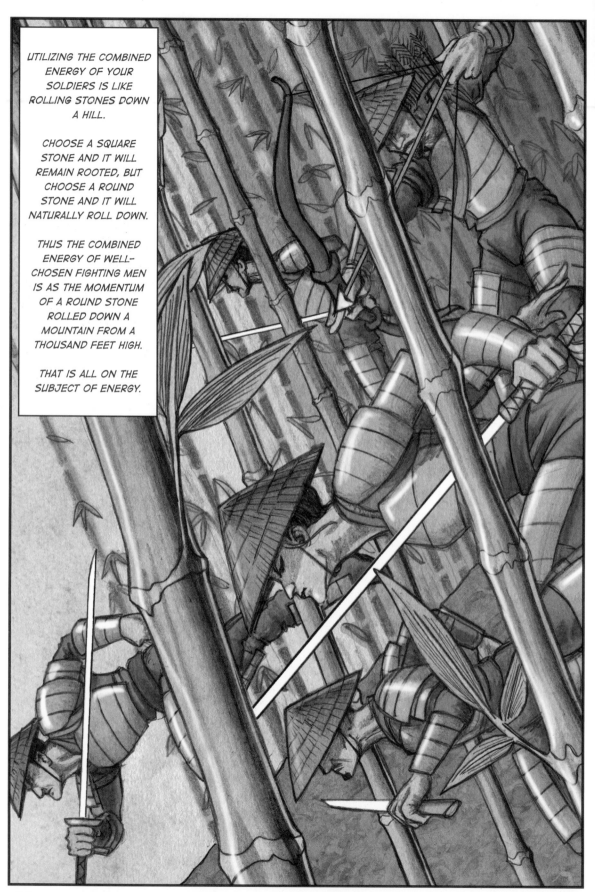

UTILIZING THE COMBINED ENERGY OF YOUR SOLDIERS IS LIKE ROLLING STONES DOWN A HILL.

CHOOSE A SQUARE STONE AND IT WILL REMAIN ROOTED, BUT CHOOSE A ROUND STONE AND IT WILL NATURALLY ROLL DOWN.

THUS THE COMBINED ENERGY OF WELL-CHOSEN FIGHTING MEN IS AS THE MOMENTUM OF A ROUND STONE ROLLED DOWN A MOUNTAIN FROM A THOUSAND FEET HIGH.

THAT IS ALL ON THE SUBJECT OF ENERGY.

WE'VE LOOKED AT "TACTICAL DISPOSITIONS," WHICH IS ATTACK AND DEFENSE, AND "ENERGY," WHICH DEALS WITH DIRECT AND INDIRECT ATTACK METHODS.

THE NEXT LESSON WILL BE ON WEAK AND STRONG POINTS. OR "TARGETS," IF YOU PREFER.

A GOOD GENERAL MUST BE WELL VERSED IN GOOD DEFENSE AND ALL FORMS OF DIRECT AND INDIRECT ATTACK BEFORE PROCEEDING TO THE SUBJECT OF WEAK AND STRONG POINTS.

THAT IS WHY "TARGETS" IS THE NEXT CHAPTER.

BUT BEFORE WE PLUNGE IN, HOW ARE YOU FINDING SUN TZU SO FAR, LIU?

IT SEEMS VERY SIMPLE YET VERY COMPLICATED AT THE SAME TIME.

A VERY FAIR ANSWER. ON THE SURFACE, MASTER TZU'S ADVICE SEEMS STRAIGHTFORWARD OR EVEN OBVIOUS, BUT OF COURSE LIFE IS NOT STRAIGHTFORWARD.

IT IS UP TO US TO TAKE HIS TEACHINGS, DRIVE THROUGH TO THE ESSENCE OF THEM, AND THEN UTILIZE THEIR WISDOM IN WHATEVER SITUATION WE FACE.

DID YOU NOTICE HOW HE SOMETIMES VEERS AWAY FROM THE CHAPTER SUBJECT AND OFTEN REPEATS SOMETHING HE HAS ALREADY EXPRESSED?

I DID.

SOME THINK THIS MAY BE A MISTAKE DUE TO BAD COPIES OF THE BOOK BEING MADE. BUT I DON'T THINK SO.

I THINK MASTER TZU IS JUST TRYING TO MAKE SURE HIS POINTS ARE CLEARLY UNDERSTOOD.

I DON'T THINK IT'S A MISTAKE EITHER.

WHY IS THAT?

OLD PEOPLE LOVE REPEATING THEMSELVES.

PART SIX

TARGETS

SUN TZU SAID: *FIRST TO THE BATTLEFIELD WAITS FOR THE ENEMY, FRESH FOR THE FIGHT.*
SECOND, HURRYING TO THE FIELD, ARRIVES EXHAUSTED.
THE CLEVER FIGHTER PROVOKES HIS ENEMY, BUT IS NOT PROVOKED.
HE CAN LURE THE ENEMY TO APPROACH OR PREVENT HIS ADVANCE.
IF YOUR ENEMY RESTS, HARASS HIM. IF WELL FED, STARVE HIM. IF ENCAMPED, ROUST HIM OUT.
APPEAR AT POINTS WHICH THE ENEMY MUST RUSH TO DEFEND; HURRY TO APPEAR WHERE YOU ARE
LEAST EXPECTED.
AN ARMY CAN MARCH GREAT LEAGUES WITH NO DISTRESS IF IT MARCHES WHERE NO ENEMY LIES.

ENSURE VICTORY BY ATTACKING POINTS UNDEFENDED.
ENSURE COMPLETE DEFENSE BY DEFENDING IMPENETRABLE POINTS.

THE SKILLFUL ATTACKER'S OPPONENT KNOWS NOT WHAT TO DEFEND; THE SKILLFUL DEFENDER'S OPPONENT KNOWS NOT WHAT TO ATTACK.

LEARN THE DIVINE ART OF SUBTLETY AND SECRECY. THIS WILL TEACH YOU TO BE INVISIBLE AND INAUDIBLE, AND HOLD THE ENEMY'S FATE IN YOUR HANDS.

ADVANCE IRRESISTIBLY, ATTACKING WEAK SPOTS. RETREAT QUICKLY, AVOIDING PURSUIT.

IF YOU WISH TO PROVOKE YOUR ENEMY INTO ACTION, ATTACK YOUR ENEMY'S WEAK PLACES.
NO MATTER HOW HIGH HIS DEFENSE WALLS OR HOW DEEP HIS MOAT, HE WILL BE FORCED TO SEND RESCUE.

IF YOU DO NOT WISH TO ENGAGE, SIMPLY DISTRACT YOUR ENEMY IN ODD AND UNACCOUNTABLE WAYS.

BY DISCOVERING THE ENEMY'S DISPOSITIONS AND REMAINING INVISIBLE, YOU CAN KEEP YOUR FORCES CONCENTRATED WHILE YOUR ENEMY MUST DIVIDE THEIRS.

YOU WILL BE A SINGLE, LARGE FORCE; YOUR OPPONENT'S WILL BE SCATTERED INTO SMALLER FORCES. YOU WILL BE MANY AGAINST HIS FEW.

KEEP YOUR POINT OF ATTACK SECRET. THAT WAY, YOUR ENEMY MUST DEFEND MANY POINTS, MAKING HIS FORCES AT EVERY POINT FEWER THAN YOURS.

IF HE STRENGTHENS HIS VANGUARD, HIS REAR WILL WEAKEN. IF HE STRENGTHENS HIS REAR, HIS VANGUARD WILL WEAKEN. IF HE STRENGTHENS HIS LEFT FLANK, HIS RIGHT WILL WEAKEN. IF HE STRENGTHENS HIS RIGHT FLANK, HIS LEFT WILL WEAKEN. IF HE SENDS HIS FORCES EVERYWHERE, HE WILL EVERYWHERE BE WEAK.

WEAKNESS COMES FROM PREPARING FOR MANY ATTACKS. STRENGTH COMES FROM FORCING THE ENEMY TO PREPARE FOR MANY ATTACKS.

KNOWING THE PLACE AND TIME OF A COMING BATTLE ENABLES THE PREPARED TO ENGAGE EASILY, EVEN AFTER A LENGTHY MARCH.
BUT IF PLACE AND TIME ARE UNKNOWN, THEN LEFT CANNOT AID RIGHT, RIGHT CANNOT AID LEFT. THE VANGUARD CANNOT SUPPORT THE REAR AND THE REAR CANNOT GIVE AID TO THE VANGUARD.

THIS IS MUCH WORSE WHEN SEPARATED BY LEAGUES OR EVEN BY A SINGLE MILE.

IMAGINE AN ARMY ADVANCING TOWARD A MEETING POINT IN SEPARATE COLUMNS, EACH WITH ORDERS TO BE THERE ON A FIXED DATE.

WITHOUT PRECISE PLANNING AND INFORMATION, THE COLUMNS WILL ADVANCE IN A HAPHAZARD MANNER WITHOUT PROPER DEFENSES.

SUDDENLY COMING UPON A POWERFUL FOE WILL MEAN ENTERING BATTLE IN A FLURRIED CONDITION.

NO MUTUAL SUPPORT WILL BE POSSIBLE BETWEEN FLANKS, VANGUARD, OR REAR, ESPECIALLY IF THE ARMY IS SPACED OUT OVER LARGE DISTANCES.

AN ARMY'S SUPERIOR NUMBERS DOES NOT ALWAYS ENSURE VICTORY. KNOWLEDGE OF BATTLE LOCATION WILL ALWAYS BRING ADVANTAGE EVEN TO THE SMALLER FORCE.

IF YOUR ENEMY IS STRONGER, YOU MAY PREVENT HIM FROM FIGHTING. PROBE HIM FOR THE DEFECTS IN HIS PLANS. ROUSE HIM TO LEARN HIS TEMPERAMENT. INSPECT HIM TO DISCOVER HIS VULNERABILITIES. CAREFULLY COMPARE YOUR ARMIES SO YOU MAY KNOW WHERE STRENGTH IS ABUNDANT AND WHERE IT IS DEFICIENT.

WHEN MAKING TACTICAL PLANS, THE MOST SKILLED BECOME UNFATHOMABLE. SHOW NO SIGNS OF WHAT YOU MEAN TO DO AND YOU WILL BE SAFE FROM THE PRYING OF THE SUBTLEST SPIES AND THE MACHINATIONS OF THE WISEST BRAINS.

VICTORY THROUGH THE MANIPULATION OF YOUR ENEMY'S TACTICS IS INCOMPREHENSIBLE TO THE COMMON MAN. HE SEES THE TACTICS USED TO CONQUER BUT CANNOT SEE THE STRATEGY OUT OF WHICH VICTORY EVOLVES.

EVERYBODY CAN SEE SUPERFICIALLY HOW A BATTLE IS WON. WHAT THEY CANNOT SEE IS THE LONG SERIES OF PLANS AND CALCULATIONS WHICH PRECEDED THE BATTLE.

DO NOT REPEAT METHODS OF VICTORY. LET YOUR METHODS BE SHAPED BY THE INFINITE VARIETY OF CIRCUMSTANCES. MILITARY TACTICS ARE LIKE WATER; FOR WATER IN ITS NATURAL COURSE RUNS AWAY FROM HIGH PLACES AND HASTENS DOWNWARD.

SO IN WAR, AVOID WHAT IS STRONG AND STRIKE AT WHAT IS WEAK.

WATER SHAPES ITS COURSE ACCORDING TO THE NATURAL OBSTACLES AROUND WHICH IT FLOWS; THE SOLDIER CREATES HIS VICTORY IN RELATION TO THE FOE HE FACES.

WATER RETAINS NO CONSTANT SHAPE, SO IN WARFARE NO CONDITIONS ARE CONSTANT.

BE FLUID AND INCONSTANT AS WATER IN YOUR TACTICS, ADAPTING THEM TO EACH SITUATION AS IT ARISES, AND YOU WILL BE A MASTER OF WAR.

AMONG THE FIVE ELEMENTS, NONE CONSTANTLY DOMINATE. THE FOUR SEASONS FOLLOW EACH OTHER IN TURN. THERE ARE SHORT DAYS AND LONG; THE MOON WAXES AND WANES.

THAT IS ALL ON WEAK AND STRONG TARGETS.

HMMMM.
THAT SOUNDS LIKE WANG
HUFFING AND PUFFING UP
THE HILL.

SIFU! SIFU! QUICK!
BANDITS HAVE ATTACKED
THE TOWN!

WHAT?!
RIGHT
NOW?

YES! MOST
PEOPLE HAVE
LOCKED THEMSELVES
IN THEIR HOMES, BUT
A FEW HAVE BEEN
CAUGHT OUT IN
THE STREET!

IT'S THE SAME BAND THAT'S
BEEN ATTACKING THE NORTHERN
VILLAGES. THEY BEAR THE STANDARD
OF THE BLACK HAND!

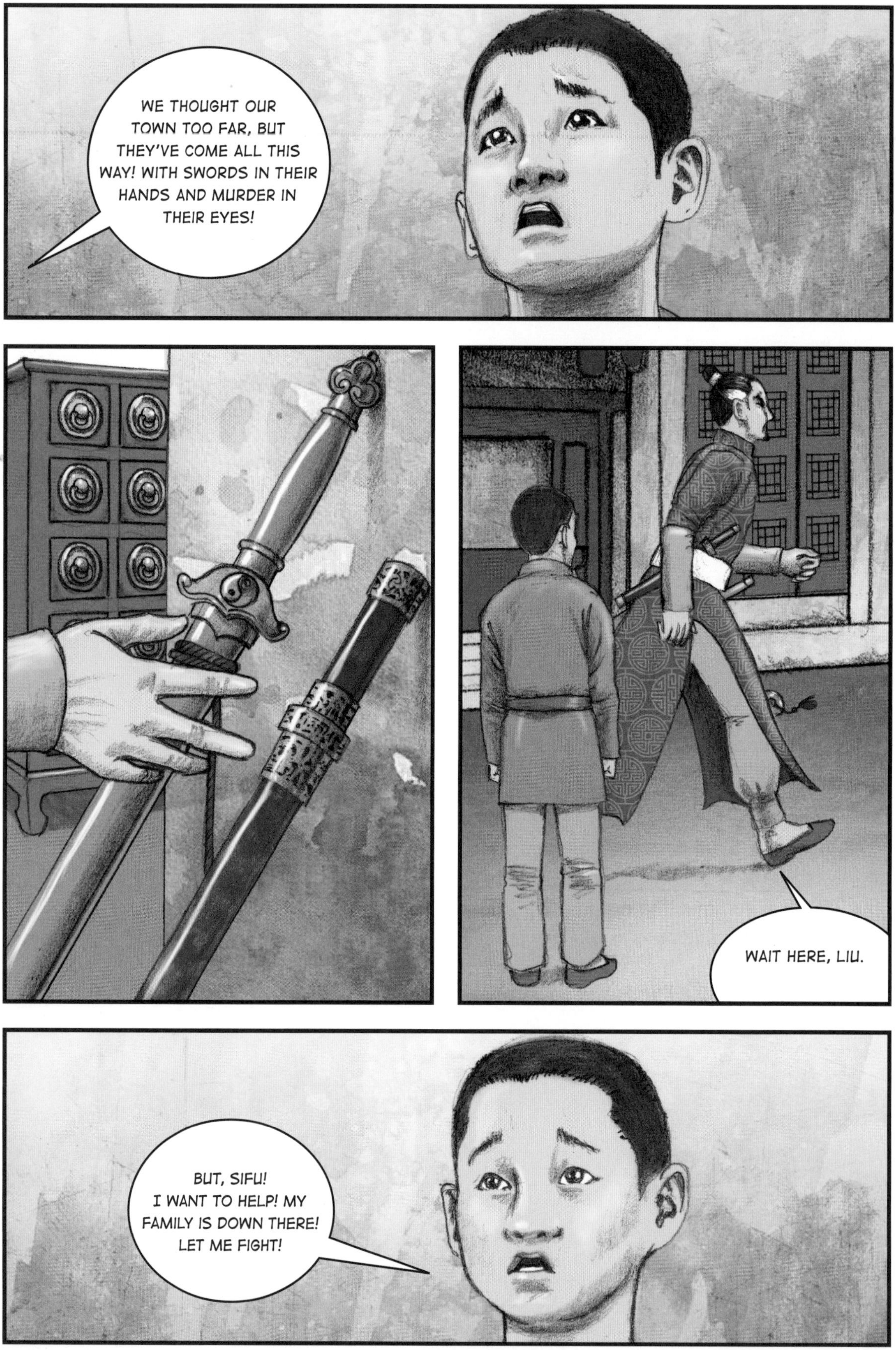
WE THOUGHT OUR TOWN TOO FAR, BUT THEY'VE COME ALL THIS WAY! WITH SWORDS IN THEIR HANDS AND MURDER IN THEIR EYES!
WAIT HERE, LIU.
BUT, SIFU! I WANT TO HELP! MY FAMILY IS DOWN THERE! LET ME FIGHT!

WHAT HELP WILL YOU BE? YOU CAN BARELY SWING A SWORD YET!

IF YOU REALLY WANT TO HELP ME, THEN DO AS I SAY AND WAIT HERE. I CAN FIGHT BETTER KNOWING I DON'T NEED TO WORRY ABOUT YOU AS WELL.

A... ALL RIGHT, SIFU. PLEASE. PLEASE SEE THAT MY FAMILY IS SAFE.

I WILL.

NOW GO INSIDE. AND IF YOU HEAR ANYTHING STRANGE, HIDE.

PART SEVEN

BATTLE MANEUVERS

SUN TZU SAID: IN WAR, THE GENERAL RECEIVES COMMANDS FROM HIS SOVEREIGN. HE COLLECTS HIS TROOPS AND FORMS HIS ARMY. HE ESTABLISHES HARMONY AND CONFIDENCE BEFORE MAKING CAMP OPPOSITE THE ENEMY. THEN THE GENUINE DIFFICULTY OF BATTLE MANEUVERS BEGINS.

THE DIFFICULTY OF BATTLE MANEUVERING IS TURNING DEVIATION TO DIRECT, AND MISFORTUNE INTO GAIN.

TAKE A MEANDERING ROUTE TO YOUR PLACE OF CHOICE, AFTER LURING THE ENEMY THERE. EVEN THOUGH IT APPEARS YOU STARTED OUT AFTER HIM, ARRIVE AT YOUR GOAL FIRST. THIS IS MASTERING DEVIATION.

MANEUVERS MAY BE PROFITABLE OR THEY MAY BE DANGEROUS; ALL DEPENDS ON THE DISCIPLINE AND ABILITY OF THE GENERAL.

LAUNCHING YOUR WHOLE ARMY INTO A MARCH FOR GAIN SACRIFICES SPEED. USING FAST TROOPS FOR GAIN USUALLY MEANS SACRIFICING EQUIPMENT AND STORES.

ORDERING YOUR MEN TO CARRY ALL THEIR EQUIPMENT AND MAKE A FORCED MARCH ACROSS MANY LEAGUES WITHOUT HALTING DAY OR NIGHT, COVERING DOUBLE THE USUAL DISTANCE, IN ORDER TO CLAIM AN ADVANTAGE, WILL RESULT IN THE LOSS OF YOUR COMMANDING OFFICERS. THE STRONGEST MEN WILL BE IN THE VANGUARD, THE TIRED ONES WILL FALL BEHIND. YOUR PLAN WILL SEE ONLY ONE IN TEN SOLDIERS ARRIVE.

MAKE THEM MARCH FIFTEEN MILES TO OUTMANEUVER YOUR ENEMY AND YOU WILL LOSE YOUR VANGUARD'S COMMANDER AND ONLY HALF YOUR MEN WILL ARRIVE. MAKE THEM MARCH TEN MILES AND TWO-THIRDS OF YOUR ARMY WILL ARRIVE.
AN ARMY WITHOUT ITS EQUIPMENT, WITHOUT ITS PROVISIONS, AND WITHOUT ITS BASES OF SUPPLY IS LOST.

  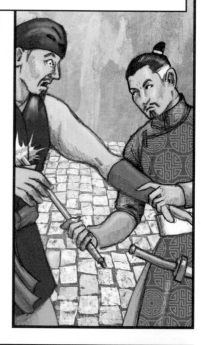

WITHOUT KNOWING YOUR NEIGHBOR'S PLANS, YOU CANNOT MAKE ALLIANCES.
WITHOUT HAVING INTIMATE KNOWLEDGE OF YOUR SURROUNDINGS—THE MOUNTAINS AND FORESTS, PITFALLS AND PRECIPICES, MARSHES AND SWAMPS—YOU CANNOT MARCH.

WITHOUT THE USE OF LOCAL GUIDES, YOU CANNOT UTILIZE THE ADVANTAGES OF YOUR SURROUNDINGS.

IN WAR, MASTERING DUPLICITY BRINGS SUCCESS. LET TROOP MOVEMENT BE DECIDED BY CIRCUMSTANCE.

BE LIKE THE WIND IN YOUR SPEED, LIKE THE FOREST IN YOUR SOLIDITY, LIKE FIRE IN YOUR ATTACK, LIKE A MOUNTAIN IN YOUR IMMOVABILITY.

LET YOUR PLANS BE IMPENETRABLE AS THE DARK, YOUR MOVEMENTS LIKE LIGHTNING.

PLUNDER THE COUNTRYSIDE AND CAPTURE NEW TERRITORY, DIVIDING THE LAND AND SPOILS AMONG YOUR TROOPS.

DELIBERATE CAREFULLY BEFORE MAKING A MOVE.

MASTER THE ART OF DUPLICITY AND VICTORY WILL BE YOURS.

SUCH IS THE ART OF BATTLE MANEUVERS.

IN BATTLE, WHEN WORDS CANNOT BE HEARD, USE GONGS AND DRUMS. WHEN VISIBILITY IS POOR, USE BANNERS AND FLAGS. GONGS AND DRUMS, BANNERS AND FLAGS ARE THE EARS AND EYES OF YOUR ARMY.

WITH YOUR ARMY UNITED AS A SINGLE BODY, YOUR BRAVEST WILL NOT ADVANCE ALONE, OR YOUR MEEKEST RETREAT ALONE. THIS IS THE ART OF HANDLING LARGE MASSES OF MEN.

IN DAYLIGHT BATTLES USE BANNERS AND FLAGS, IN NIGHT BATTLES USE TORCHES AND DRUMS. SO YOUR TROOPS ARE NEVER WITHOUT DIRECTION.

A WHOLE ARMY MAY BE ROBBED OF ITS SPIRIT; A COMMANDER MAY BE ROBBED OF HIS PRESENCE OF MIND.

A SOLDIER'S SPIRIT IS KEENEST IN THE MORNING, BY NOON IT HAS WANED, AND BY EVENING HIS MIND THINKS ONLY OF REST AND HOME. A CLEVER GENERAL AVOIDS A KEEN-SPIRITED ARMY AND ATTACKS THE TIRED AND HOMESICK. THIS IS THE ART OF STUDYING MOOD.

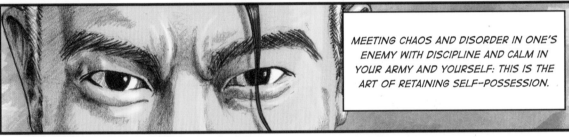

MEETING CHAOS AND DISORDER IN ONE'S ENEMY WITH DISCIPLINE AND CALM IN YOUR ARMY AND YOURSELF: THIS IS THE ART OF RETAINING SELF-POSSESSION.

TO CROSS LARGE DISTANCES AHEAD OF YOUR ENEMY, TO BE AT EASE WHILE THE ENEMY TOILS, TO BE WELL FED WHEN YOUR ENEMY STARVES. THIS IS THE ART OF REGULATING ONE'S STRENGTH.

REFRAIN FROM INTERCEPTING AN ENEMY WHOSE BANNERS ARE WELL ORDERED. REFRAIN FROM ATTACKING AN ENEMY WITH A CALM AND CONFIDENT DISPOSITION. THIS IS THE ART OF STUDYING CIRCUMSTANCE.

IN WARFARE, THESE AXIOMS ARE KNOWN: DO NOT ADVANCE UPHILL AGAINST AN ENEMY, NOR OPPOSE ONE ADVANCING DOWN.

DO NOT PURSUE AN ENEMY SIMULATING FLIGHT. DO NOT ATTACK SOLDIERS WHOSE TEMPER IS KEEN.

DO NOT SWALLOW BAIT OFFERED BY THE ENEMY.

DO NOT INTERFERE WITH AN ARMY RETURNING HOME.

WHEN SURROUNDING AN ARMY, LEAVE A PASSAGE FREE.

DO NOT PRESS A DESPERATE FOE TOO HARD.

SUCH IS THE ART OF WARFARE.

THAT IS ALL ON BATTLE MANEUVERS.

"DO NOT INTERFERE WITH AN ARMY RETURNING HOME."

I SUPPOSE A MAN WILL FIGHT MORE DESPERATELY IF HE THINKS THERE IS NO WAY OUT AND HE IS GOING TO DIE. OR WILL FIGHT MUCH HARDER TO RETURN HOME THAN TOWARD AN UNKNOWN MARK.

OF COURSE A MAN WILL FIGHT HARDER TO GET HOME.

AND THAT'S WHAT I SHOULD BE DOING. HELPING DEFEND MY HOME! I'M SORRY, SIFU. I KNOW I PROMISED TO DO AS YOU ASKED...

...BUT I MUST KNOW WHAT'S HAPPENED.

AH!

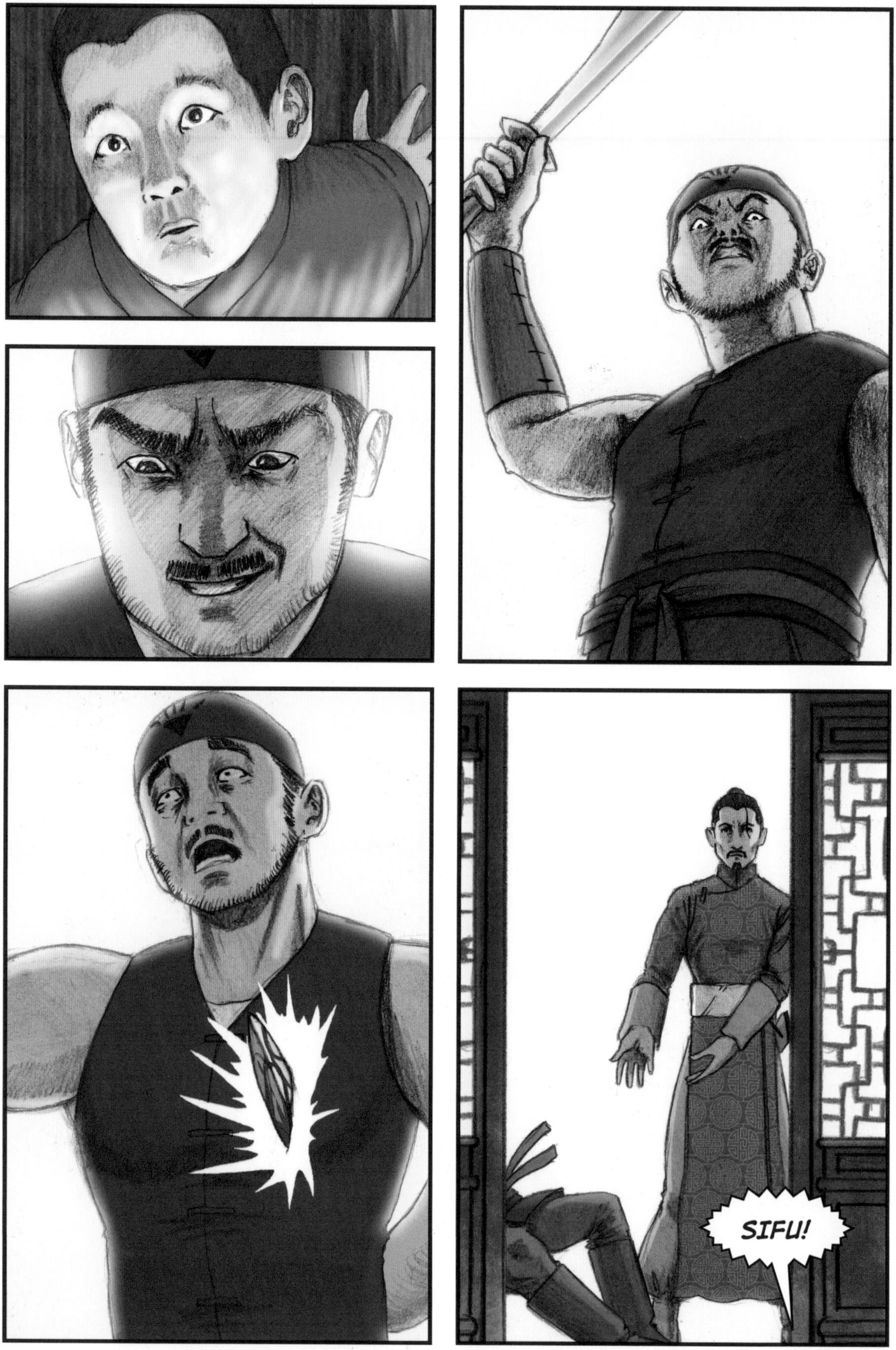
SIFU!

=PANT, PANT=
GODS, I'M TOO
OLD FOR THIS.

MY APOLOGIES, LIU. I
DIDN'T WANT TO FIGHT
HIM ON THE SLOPE, SO I
FOLLOWED HIM.

HE THOUGHT TO EVADE
ME HERE, NOT KNOWING IT
WAS MY HOUSE HE RAN TO, THE
FOOL. A VERY GOOD EXAMPLE OF A
CARELESS, UNINFORMED ENEM—

SIFU! WHAT OF
MY FAMILY?!

BE CALM, BOY.
THEY ARE A BIT
SHAKEN UP BUT
OTHERWISE FINE. WE
LOST A FEW PEOPLE,
THOUGH. MR. CHEN
AND MRS. HUANG
AMONG THEM.

A SAD
DAY INDEED.

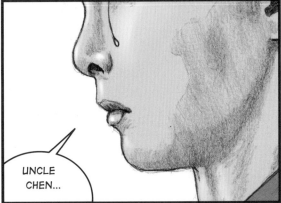

UNCLE
CHEN...

PART EIGHT

TACTICAL VARIATIONS

TODAY WE'LL BE LEARNING TACTICAL VARIATIONS. SOME PEOPLE CALL THIS CHAPTER "THE NINE VARIATIONS" TO LINK IT TO A CHAPTER FURTHER ON.

BUT NINE IS JUST A SYMBOLIC NUMBER WHICH STANDS FOR AN INDEFINITELY LARGE NUMBER OF VARIATIONS. LET US BEGIN...

SUN TZU SAID: WHILE MARCHING THROUGH CROSSROADS, JOIN FORCES WITH ALLIES. ON BARREN OR DIFFICULT LAND, DO NOT MAKE CAMP. IN DANGEROUS, ISOLATED SPOTS, DO NOT LINGER. ON HEMMED-IN GROUND, YOU MUST RESORT TO STRATAGEM. ON HOSTILE GROUND, YOU MUST FIGHT.

THERE ARE ROADS THAT MUST NOT BE FOLLOWED, ARMIES THAT MUST NOT BE ATTACKED, TOWNS WHICH MUST NOT BE BESIEGED, POSITIONS THAT MUST NOT BE CONTESTED, AND COMMANDS OF THE SOVEREIGN THAT MUST NOT BE OBEYED.

THE GENERAL WHO TRULY UNDERSTANDS THE ADVANTAGES OF TACTICAL VARIATION UNDERSTANDS WAR.

THE GENERAL WHO DOES NOT FULLY UNDERSTAND TACTICAL VARIATION, MAY BE WELL ACQUAINTED WITH THE LAY OF THE LAND BUT LACKS THE VERSATILITY OF MIND TO USE THE KNOWLEDGE TO HIS ADVANTAGE.

SO, THE STUDENT OF WAR, OBLIVIOUS TO TACTICAL VARIATION, MAY KNOW THE FIVE ADVANTAGES, BUT WILL STILL FAIL TO GAIN THE MOST FROM HIS MEN.

THE FIVE ADVANTAGES ARE THESE: IF A ROAD IS SHORT, FOLLOW IT. IF AN ARMY IS ISOLATED, ATTACK IT. IF A TOWN IS IN A PRECARIOUS CONDITION, BESIEGE IT.

IF A POSITION CAN BE STORMED, ATTEMPT IT. AND IF CONSISTENT WITH MILITARY OPERATIONS, THE RULER'S COMMAND MUST BE OBEYED.

GIVE ME AN EXAMPLE WHEN YOU WOULD VARY FROM THESE RULES.

IF THE ROAD WAS SHORT, BUT YOU KNEW THAT AN AMBUSH WAITED ALONG IT, YOU WOULD TAKE ANOTHER, LONGER ROAD?

VERY GOOD, LIU.

THE WISE LEADER MUST
CONSIDER NOT ONLY
THE ADVANTAGES AND
GAINS, BUT ALSO THE
DISADVANTAGES
AND LOSSES.

TEMPERING HIS
EXPECTATIONS THIS WAY
WILL ENSURE HE CAN
SUCCEED IN HIS PLANS.

ADVERSELY, TEMPERING
THOUGHTS OF DAMAGE
WITH POTENTIAL
ADVANTAGE MAY
ENABLE ESCAPE
FROM MISFORTUNE.

SUBDUE HOSTILE LORDS
BY INFLICTING DAMAGE
ON THEM, HARASS
THEM AND KEEP THEM
OCCUPIED, MAKE THEM
RUSH TO ANY GIVEN
POINT WITH BAITS
AND LURES.

THE ART OF WAR
TEACHES US NOT TO
RELY ON THE ENEMY'S
FAILURE TO APPEAR
BUT ON OUR OWN
READINESS TO RECEIVE
HIM; NOT ON THE
ENEMY'S FAILURE TO
ATTACK BUT RATHER OUR
OWN UNASSAILABLE
AND VARIED DEFENSES.

THERE ARE FIVE PERSONALITY PITFALLS FOR A GENERAL:

RECKLESSNESS, WHICH LEADS TO DESTRUCTION.

COWARDICE, WHICH LEADS TO CAPTURE.

A HOT TEMPER, WHICH IS EASILY PROVOKED.

A DELICACY OF HONOR, SUSCEPTIBLE TO SHAME.

OVERCONCERN FOR HIS MEN, WHICH EXPOSES HIM TO WORRY AND TROUBLE.

THESE FIVE DEFECTS IN A GENERAL ARE RUINOUS TO THE PLANS OF WAR.

WHEN AN ARMY IS OVERTHROWN AND ITS LEADER SLAIN, THE CAUSE WILL SURELY BE ONE OF THESE FIVE FAULTS.

LET THEM BE THE SUBJECT OF MEDITATION.

MASTER TZU DOESN'T MEAN A GENERAL SHOULD NEGLECT HIS TROOPS. HE WISHES TO EMPHASIZE THE DANGER OF SACRIFICING ANY IMPORTANT MILITARY ADVANTAGE TO THE IMMEDIATE COMFORT OF HIS MEN.

THIS IS SHORT-SIGHTED, AS WHATEVER AILS HIS TROOPS IN THE SHORT TERM WILL BE NOTHING TO THE SUFFERING OF OVERALL DEFEAT.

WHY DID THE BANDITS ATTACK US, SIFU?

WHY MUST THERE ALWAYS BE FIGHTING AND SADNESS? WHY DO MEN DO THIS?

THERE WILL ALWAYS BE THOSE WHO PREFER TAKING WHAT THEY NEED FROM OTHERS, RATHER THAN WORKING FOR IT THEMSELVES.

THE IMPERIAL ARMY CAN'T BE EVERYWHERE. THESE ARE DIFFICULT AND BRUTAL TIMES WE LIVE IN.

I HATE IT. I HATE THAT WE CAN NEVER FEEL SAFE.

WHEN I'M OLDER AND STRONG ENOUGH I WILL PROTECT THE ORDINARY PEOPLE. I'LL PUT A STOP TO THE RAIDERS, THE PIRATES, THE STEALING, AND THE KILLING.

I DON'T DOUBT IT. BUT BETWEEN THEN AND NOW ARE A LOT OF YEARS AND MUCH LEARNING TO BE DONE.

WHICH WE'LL CONTINUE TOMORROW. NOW RUN HOME AND GET SOME DINNER IN YOU.

PART NINE

ON THE MARCH

SUN TZU SAID: *NOW WE COME TO ENCAMPING YOUR ARMY AND OBSERVING SIGNS OF THE ENEMY. IN HIGH COUNTRY, PASS OVER MOUNTAINS QUICKLY AND STAY NEAR VALLEYS. CAMP IN HIGH PLACES, FACING SOUTH OR EAST. DO NOT FIGHT UPHILL, FIGHT DOWN. THIS IS MOUNTAIN WARFARE.*

IN WET COUNTRY, CROSS RIVERS, THEN DISTANCE YOURSELF FROM THEM. WHEN YOUR ENEMY APPROACHES YOU ACROSS A RIVER, DO NOT MEET THEM MIDSTREAM. LET HALF THE ARMY CROSS, THEN DELIVER YOUR ATTACK. IF YOU WISH TO FIGHT, DO NOT APPROACH THE RIVER BUT HOLD POSITION ON HIGHER GROUND. DO NOT MOVE UPSTREAM AGAINST THE FLOW TO ENGAGE THE ENEMY. THIS IS RIVER WARFARE.

IN SALT-MARSH COUNTRY, CROSS QUICKLY, WITHOUT DELAY.

IF FORCED TO FIGHT IN THESE AREAS, BATTLE NEAR FRESH WATER AND GRASS, WITH TREES BEHIND YOU. THIS IS SALT-MARSH WARFARE.

THE GROUND NEAR TREES WILL BE MORE SECURE THAN MOST MARSHLAND AND THE TREES WILL SHIELD YOUR REAR.

IN DRY, LEVEL COUNTRY, TAKE POSITION ON EASY GROUND. KEEP RISING GROUND TO YOUR REAR, SO THAT THE DANGER LIES AHEAD, AND SAFETY BEHIND. THIS IS FLAT LAND WARFARE.

THESE FOUR USEFUL BRANCHES OF MILITARY KNOWLEDGE ENABLED THE YELLOW EMPEROR TO VANQUISH FOUR OTHER SOVEREIGNS.

ALL ARMIES PREFER HIGH GROUND TO LOW, SUNNY PLACES TO DARK.

IF YOU ARE CAREFUL OF YOUR MEN AND CAMP ON HARD GROUND, THEY WILL BE FREE FROM DISEASE OF EVERY KIND, AND THIS WILL SPELL VICTORY.

WHEN YOU COME TO HILL OR BANK, OCCUPY THE SUNNY SIDE, WITH THE RISE TO YOUR REAR. THIS WILL UTILIZE THE GROUND'S NATURAL ADVANTAGE TO THE BENEFIT OF YOUR TROOPS.

IF A RIVER YOU WISH TO CROSS IS SWOLLEN FROM RAIN, WAIT UNTIL IT SUBSIDES.

WHEN ENCOUNTERING PRECIPITOUS CLIFFS WITH TORRENTS RUNNING BETWEEN, DEEP NATURAL HOLLOWS, CONFINED PLACES, TANGLED THICKETS, QUAGMIRES, AND CREVASSES, DO NOT APPROACH. CAUSE THE ENEMY TO APPROACH SUCH PLACES SO AS YOU FACE THEM, SO THE DANGERS ARE AT THEIR BACK.

IF YOU FIND YOURSELF NEAR HILLY COUNTRY, OVERGROWN PONDS, REEDY MARSH, OR DENSE WOODS, SEARCH THEM CAREFULLY; FOR THESE ARE PLACES THAT HOUSE AMBUSHERS OR SPIES.

WHEN THE ENEMY IS CLOSE AT HAND BUT REMAINS QUIET, HE TRUSTS IN HIS STRONG POSITION.

WHEN HE KEEPS HIS DISTANCE BUT TRIES TO PROVOKE A BATTLE, HE DESIRES YOUR ADVANCE.

IF HIS CAMP IS EASY TO ACCESS, HE IS LURING YOU.

MOVEMENT AMONG TREES BETRAYS THE ENEMY ADVANCING.

THE SIGHT OF MANY SCREENS IN THE MIDST OF THICK GRASS MEANS THE ENEMY WANTS TO MAKE YOU SUSPICIOUS.

THE RISING OF BIRDS IN THEIR FLIGHT OR STARTLED BEASTS INDICATE AN IMMINENT AMBUSH.

THE PRESENCE OF A NUMBER OF SCREENS OR SHEDS IN THE MIDST OF THICK VEGETATION IS A SURE SIGN THAT THE ENEMY HAS FLED...

...AND FEARING PURSUIT, HAS BUILT THESE FALSE HIDING PLACES TO TRY TO FOOL THEIR ENEMY INTO SUSPECTING AN AMBUSH, THUS SLOWING THEM DOWN.

WHEN YOU OBSERVE DUST RISING HIGH, IT SIGNIFIES CHARIOTS ADVANCING.

WHEN THE DUST IS LOW, BUT SPREAD OVER A WIDE AREA, IT SIGNIFIES THE APPROACH OF INFANTRY.

WHEN IT BRANCHES OUT IN DIFFERENT DIRECTIONS, IT SHOWS PARTIES SENT OUT FOR FIREWOOD COLLECTION.

A FEW CLOUDS WAFTING TO AND FRO SIGNIFY THE ARMY IS ENCAMPING.

HUMBLE WORDS BUT INCREASED PREPARATIONS ARE A SIGN OF IMMINENT ATTACK. VIOLENT WORDS AND A THREATENING ADVANCE MASK A LIKELY RETREAT.

PEACE PROPOSALS UNACCOMPANIED BY A SIGNED TREATY INDICATE A PLOT.

LIGHT CHARIOTS APPEARING FIRST AND TAKING POSITION ON THE WINGS ARE A SIGN THE ENEMY IS FORMING FOR BATTLE.
MUCH RUNNING ABOUT AND SOLDIERS FALLING INTO RANK MEANS THAT THE CRITICAL MOMENT HAS COME.
WHEN SOME ARE SEEN ADVANCING AND SOME RETREATING, IT IS A LURE.

WHEN SOLDIERS STAND LEANING ON THEIR SPEARS, THEY ARE WEAK FROM HUNGER. IF WATER BEARERS DRINK FIRST, THE ARMY IS SUFFERING FROM THIRST. IF AN ADVANTAGE IS CLEAR BUT NOT ACTED UPON, THE SOLDIERS ARE EXHAUSTED.

IF BIRDS GATHER ON ANY SPOT, IT IS UNOCCUPIED.

SHOUTING AT NIGHT SIGNIFIES NERVOUSNESS. DISTURBANCES IN CAMP SIGNIFY WEAK AUTHORITY. SHIFTING BANNERS AND FLAGS SIGNIFY DISORDER. ANGRY OFFICERS SIGNIFY WEARY SOLDIERS.

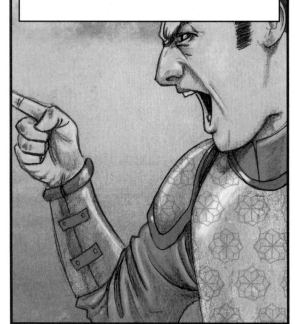

WHEN AN ARMY KILLS ITS ANIMALS FOR FOOD AND THE MEN DO NOT SET UP FIRES TO RETURN TO, THIS IS THE SUREST SIGN THEY ARE PREPARING TO FIGHT TO THE DEATH.

MEN WHISPERING IN SMALL KNOTS POINTS TO DISCONTENT.

COPIOUS REWARDS SIGNIFY FEAR; COPIOUS PUNISHMENTS SIGNIFY DIRE DISTRESS.

BEGINNING WITH BRAVADO THAT TURNS TO FEAR AT TROOP NUMBERS SHOWS A SUPREME LACK OF INTELLIGENCE.

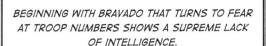

WHEN ENVOYS APPROACH WITH HONEY-COVERED WORDS, IT IS A SIGN THE ENEMY WISHES FOR RESPITE OR A TRUCE.

IF AGGRESSIVE ENEMY TROOPS ADVANCE AND REMAIN FACING YOURS FOR A PROTRACTED PERIOD WITHOUT ATTACK OR RETREAT, REMAIN DEEPLY VIGILANT.

AN ARMY EQUAL IN NUMBER TO YOUR ENEMY'S IS ENOUGH. DIRECT ATTACK IS ILL-ADVISED BUT CONCENTRATE YOUR STRENGTH, SCRUTINIZE YOUR ENEMY, AND IF POSSIBLE, OBTAIN REINFORCEMENTS.

EXERCISING NO FORETHOUGHT AND RIDICULING YOUR OPPONENTS WILL LEAD TO YOUR CAPTURE.

PUNISHING SOLDIERS BEFORE THEY ARE LOYAL WILL MAKE THEM UNRULY. BUT LET LOYAL SOLDIERS GO UNPUNISHED AND THEY WILL BECOME EQUALLY USELESS.

TREAT SOLDIERS WITH DISCIPLINE BUT RESPECT. THIS WILL GARNER CONFIDENCE. CONSISTENCY IN COMMAND INSPIRES OBEDIENCE; INCONSISTENCY INSPIRES INSUBORDINATION.

A GENERAL CONFIDENT IN HIS MEN'S STRENGTH AND ACQUIESCENCE INSPIRES MUTUAL TRUST.

THE ART OF GIVING ORDERS IS NOT TO TRY TO RECTIFY MINOR BLUNDERS AND NOT TO BE SWAYED BY PETTY DOUBTS. HESITATION AND FUSSINESS ARE THE SUREST MEANS OF SAPPING THE CONFIDENCE OF AN ARMY.

IT MUST BE SCARY, THOUGH, TO LEAD A WHOLE ARMY.

OF COURSE IT IS. ANYONE THAT SAYS OTHERWISE IS EITHER ARROGANT OR A FOOL. BUT TAKE THE TIME TO GET TO KNOW YOUR MEN AND THEIR TALENTS, AND YOUR CONFIDENCE WILL RISE.

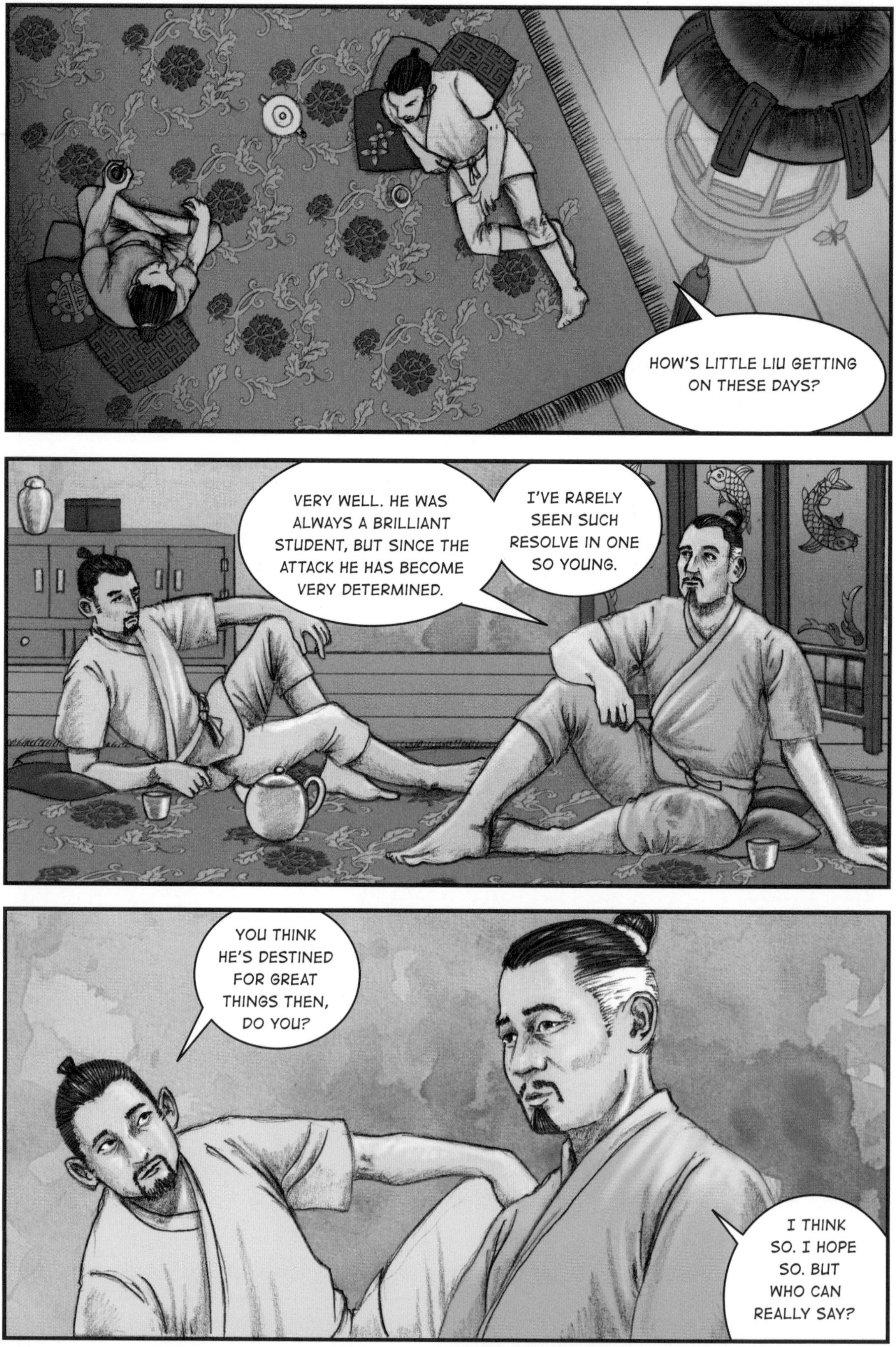
HOW'S LITTLE LIU GETTING ON THESE DAYS?
VERY WELL. HE WAS ALWAYS A BRILLIANT STUDENT, BUT SINCE THE ATTACK HE HAS BECOME VERY DETERMINED.
I'VE RARELY SEEN SUCH RESOLVE IN ONE SO YOUNG.
YOU THINK HE'S DESTINED FOR GREAT THINGS THEN, DO YOU?
I THINK SO. I HOPE SO. BUT WHO CAN REALLY SAY?

EXACTLY! SO WHY BOTHER? HE MIGHT FALL IN A WELL TOMORROW.

WHY PUT ALL THIS EFFORT INTO HIS EDUCATION? HE'S NOT YOUR SON. YOU COULD BE FISHING OR HUNTING, OR TRAVELING WITH ME.

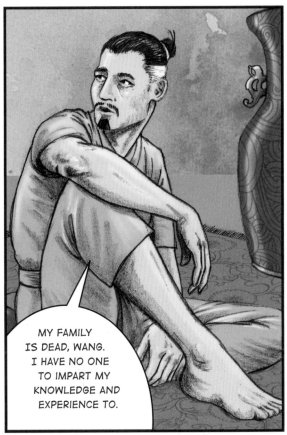

MY FAMILY IS DEAD, WANG. I HAVE NO ONE TO IMPART MY KNOWLEDGE AND EXPERIENCE TO.

I'VE FOUND A BOY WHO MAY WELL MAKE A DIFFERENCE TO OUR COUNTRY'S FUTURE IF GUIDED PROPERLY. I'M SATISFIED KNOWING I'M DOING THE RIGHT THING.

BEFORE YOU LEAVE THIS LIFE, DON'T YOU WANT TO LEAVE YOUR MARK, YOUR LEGACY?

I'LL LEAVE THE FAME AND RENOWN TO YOU, MY FRIEND. ANONYMITY IS MORE ME.

BESIDES, MEN OF MYSTERY ARE FAR MORE ATTRACTIVE.

PART TEN

TERRAIN

SUN TZU SAID: *THERE ARE MORE OR LESS SIX KINDS OF TERRAIN: ACCESSIBLE GROUND, ENTANGLING GROUND, STANDOFF GROUND, CLOSED-IN GROUND, PRECIPITOUS GROUND, AND DISTANT GROUND.*

ACCESSIBLE GROUND ENABLES BOTH SIDES TO MOVE ABOUT FREELY.
ON THIS TYPE OF GROUND, OCCUPY HIGH GROUND AND SECURE YOUR SUPPLY LINE BEFORE THE ENEMY TO FIGHT WITH THE ADVANTAGE.

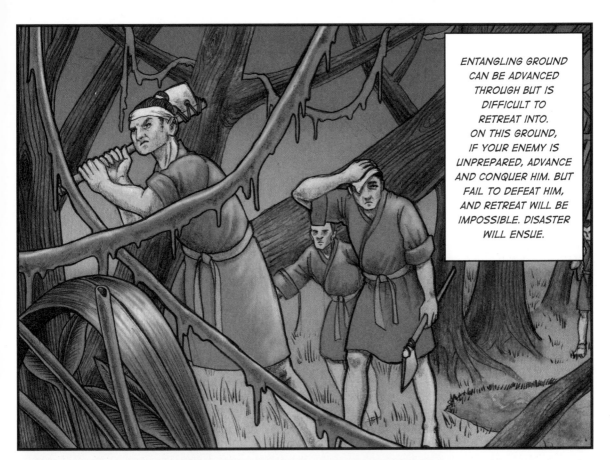

ENTANGLING GROUND CAN BE ADVANCED THROUGH BUT IS DIFFICULT TO RETREAT INTO. ON THIS GROUND, IF YOUR ENEMY IS UNPREPARED, ADVANCE AND CONQUER HIM. BUT FAIL TO DEFEAT HIM, AND RETREAT WILL BE IMPOSSIBLE. DISASTER WILL ENSUE.

STANDOFF GROUND MEANS NEITHER SIDE WILL GAIN BY MAKING THE FIRST MOVE. ON THIS TYPE OF GROUND, EVEN IF THE ENEMY OFFERS BAIT, DO NOT STIR FORTH BUT RATHER RETREAT, THUS ENTICING THE ENEMY INSTEAD; THEN, WHEN PART OF HIS ARMY HAS COME OUT, ATTACK TO YOUR ADVANTAGE.

CLOSED-IN GROUND IS NARROW PASSES AND VALLEYS. IF YOU CAN OCCUPY THEM FIRST, BAR THEM AND WAIT FOR THE ENEMY. SHOULD THE ENEMY BEAT YOU IN OCCUPYING A PASS, ONLY GO AFTER HIM IF THEY HAVE NOT BARRED IT.

ON PRECIPITOUS
GROUND, IF YOU
ARRIVE BEFORE YOUR
ADVERSARY, OCCUPY
THE RAISED SPOTS, AND
WAIT FOR HIM TO COME
UP. IF THE ENEMY HAS
OCCUPIED THE HIGH
GROUND BEFORE YOU,
DO NOT ASCEND TO HIM,
BUT RETREAT AND TRY
TO ENTICE HIM AWAY.

ON DISTANT GROUND,
IF YOU ARE SITUATED
FAR FROM THE
ENEMY, AND YOU ARE
WELL MATCHED, IT IS
DIFFICULT TO PROVOKE
A BATTLE, AND FIGHTING
WILL BE TO
YOUR DISADVANTAGE.

THESE ARE THE SIX
PRINCIPLES OF TERRAIN.
THE WISE GENERAL WILL
STUDY THEM CLOSELY.

AN ARMY IS EXPOSED TO CERTAIN CALAMITIES WHERE THE FAULT LIES WITH THE GENERAL. THESE ARE: FLIGHT, INSUBORDINATION, COLLAPSE, RUIN, DISORDER, AND ROUT.

OTHER CONDITIONS BEING EQUAL, IF ONE FORCE IS HURLED AGAINST ANOTHER TEN TIMES ITS SIZE, THE RESULT WILL BE THE FLIGHT OF THE FORMER.

WHEN THE COMMON SOLDIERS ARE TOO STRONG AND THEIR OFFICERS TOO WEAK, THE RESULT IS INSUBORDINATION.

WHEN THE OFFICERS ARE TOO STRONG AND THE COMMON SOLDIERS TOO WEAK, THE RESULT IS COLLAPSE.

WHEN ANGRY AND INSUBORDINATE, HIGHER OFFICERS CHARGE AT THE ENEMY WITH NAUGHT BUT RAGE; BEFORE THE GENERAL CAN PROPERLY GAUGE VICTORY, THE RESULT IS RUIN.

WHEN THE GENERAL IS WEAK AND WITHOUT AUTHORITY, WHEN HIS ORDERS ARE UNCLEAR AND THERE ARE NO FIXED DUTIES FOR OFFICERS AND MEN, AND RANKS ARE FORMED IN A SLOVENLY, HAPHAZARD MANNER, THE RESULT IS UTTER DISORDER.

WHEN A GENERAL, UNABLE TO ESTIMATE THE ENEMY'S STRENGTH, PITS AN INFERIOR FORCE AGAINST A LARGER ONE, OR HURLS A WEAK DETACHMENT AGAINST A POWERFUL ONE, AND NEGLECTS TO SELECT A PROPER VANGUARD, THE RESULT MUST BE ROUT.

THESE ARE SIX WAYS OF COURTING DEFEAT, WHICH EVERY GENERAL MUST HEAVILY CONSIDER.

THE FORMATION OF TERRAIN IS THE SOLDIER'S BEST AID, BUT THE POWER OF ESTIMATING THE ADVERSARY, OF UNDERSTANDING VICTORY, AND OF CALCULATING DIFFICULTIES, DANGERS, AND DISTANCES, IS THE BEST AID OF A GENERAL.

HE WHO KNOWS THIS AND UTILIZES IT DURING BATTLE WILL SURELY SUCCEED. HE WHO NEITHER KNOWS NOR DEMONSTRATES THIS KNOWLEDGE WILL SURELY BE DEFEATED.

IF FIGHTING IS SURE TO BRING VICTORY BUT YOUR RULER FORBIDS IT, FIGHT. IF FIGHTING WILL RESULT IN DEFEAT AND YET YOUR RULER ORDERS YOU TO, DO NOT.

THE GENERAL WHO ADVANCES WITHOUT COVETING FAME AND RETREATS WITHOUT FEARING DISGRACE, WHOSE ONLY THOUGHT IS TO PROTECT HIS COUNTRY AND SERVE HIS SOVEREIGN, IS THE JEWEL OF THE KINGDOM.

HIS SOLDIERS ARE HIS CHILDREN, AND THEY FOLLOW HIM INTO THE DEEPEST VALLEYS. HE LOOKS UPON THEM AS BELOVED SONS, AND THEY WILL STAND BY HIM TILL DEATH.

IF, HOWEVER, HE IS INDULGENT, BUT HAS NO AUTHORITY; KIND-HEARTED, BUT NOT COMMANDING; AND INCAPABLE OF KEEPING ORDER, THEN HIS SOLDIERS WILL BE LIKE SPOILED CHILDREN— USELESS FOR ANY PRACTICAL PURPOSE.

MASTER TZU SAYS TO DISOBEY THE LORDS? BUT, SIFU, WE ARE ALWAYS TOLD TO OBEY THE LORDS NO MATTER WHAT.

THIS IS TRUE IN MOST RESPECTS. BUT SAY YOUR ARMY IS FOUR HUNDRED MILES AWAY FROM YOUR LORD. INFORMATION TAKES TIME TO GO BACK AND FORTH.

HE WILL NOT KNOW THE CURRENT SITUATION AND WILL BE GIVING ORDERS ACCORDING TO OLD NEWS. THE GENERAL IS THE MILITARY LEADER, SO MUST ACT ON HIS OWN COUNSEL.

THERE IS A FAMOUS SAYING: "DECREES FROM THE SON OF HEAVEN DO NOT PENETRATE THE WALLS OF A CAMP."

IF WE KNOW THAT OUR OWN MEN ARE FIT FOR AN ATTACK, BUT ARE UNAWARE OF THE ENEMY'S STRENGTH, WE HAVE HALF A CHANCE OF WINNING.

IF WE KNOW THE ENEMY IS VULNERABLE, BUT ARE UNAWARE OF THE CONDITION OF OUR OWN MEN, WE HAVE HALF A CHANCE OF WINNING.

IF WE KNOW THAT THE ENEMY IS VULNERABLE, AND ALSO KNOW THAT OUR MEN ARE FIT TO ATTACK, BUT ARE UNAWARE THAT THE GROUND IS POOR FOR AN ATTACK, WE STILL ONLY HAVE HALF A CHANCE OF WINNING.

THE VETERAN SOLDIER WHO GRASPS ALL OF THIS ONCE ENGAGED NEED NEVER HESITATE. KNOWLEDGE OF YOUR ENEMY, KNOWLEDGE OF YOURSELF, KNOWLEDGE OF THE SEASONS OF HEAVEN, AND THE NATURAL ADVANTAGES OF EARTH WILL ENSURE VICTORY IN ALL YOUR BATTLES.

THIS IS ALL ON TERRAIN.

ARGH!

CHANG!

LITTLE LIU. OFF TO SEE THE FANCY MAN ON THE HILL AS USUAL?

GIMME YOUR LUNCH. OR YOU CAN TRY SOME OF THOSE FAMOUS SKILLS YOU'RE SUPPOSED TO BE LEARNING.

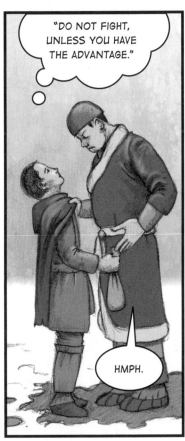

"DO NOT FIGHT, UNLESS YOU HAVE THE ADVANTAGE."

HMPH.

I BET YOU'RE NOT LEARNING TO FIGHT AT ALL! I BET YOU'RE UP THERE CLEANING HIS TOILET!

A LITTLE LATER...

CHANG! SO IT'S TRUE! SOMEONE TOLD ME YOU'VE BEEN STEALING MY PORK BUNS AND HERE YOU ARE *STUFFING YOUR FACE!*

JUST WAIT TILL I TELL YOUR PARENTS, YOU BRAT!

NOOOO!

"THE SKILLFUL LEADER BEATS HIS ENEMY WITHOUT ANY FIGHTING."

PART ELEVEN

THE NINE SITUATIONS

SUN TZU SAID: MILITARY KNOWLEDGE RECOGNIZES NINE TYPES OF POSITION: SCATTERING, SIMPLE, CONTENTIOUS, OPEN, INTERSECTING, HEAVY, TOUGH, CONFINED, AND DIRE.

WHEN A GENERAL FIGHTS IN HIS OWN LAND, IT IS A SCATTERING POSITION.
IF YOU ARE SITUATED HERE, AVOID FIGHTING.

IT IS CALLED SCATTERING BECAUSE SOLDIERS STILL NEAR THEIR HOMES WILL USE THE CHAOS OF BATTLE AS AN OPPORTUNITY TO SCATTER AND FLEE TO THEIR ANXIOUS FAMILIES.

WHICH IS EXACTLY WHAT YOU ALMOST DID WHEN THE BLACK HAND ATTACKED.

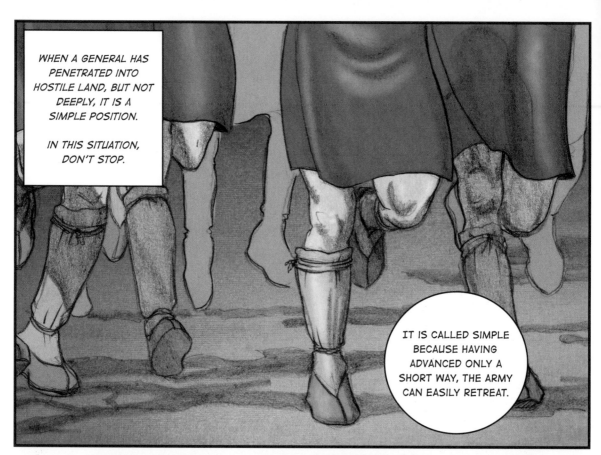

WHEN A GENERAL HAS PENETRATED INTO HOSTILE LAND, BUT NOT DEEPLY, IT IS A SIMPLE POSITION.

IN THIS SITUATION, DON'T STOP.

IT IS CALLED SIMPLE BECAUSE HAVING ADVANCED ONLY A SHORT WAY, THE ARMY CAN EASILY RETREAT.

GROUND THAT OFFERS GREAT ADVANTAGE TO EITHER SIDE IS A CONTENTIOUS POSITION.

HERE, HOLD YOUR ATTACK, STAY WARY.

GROUND ON WHICH EACH SIDE CAN EASILY MOVE IS AN OPEN POSITION.

HERE, DO NOT ATTEMPT TO BLOCK YOUR ENEMY, AS THEY HAVE THE SPACE TO OUTMANEUVER YOU.

GROUND THAT BORDERS THREE STATES, SO THAT HE WHO OCCUPIES IT FIRST HAS ACCESS TO MUCH, IS AN INTERSECTING POSITION.

HERE, JOIN WITH ALLIES.

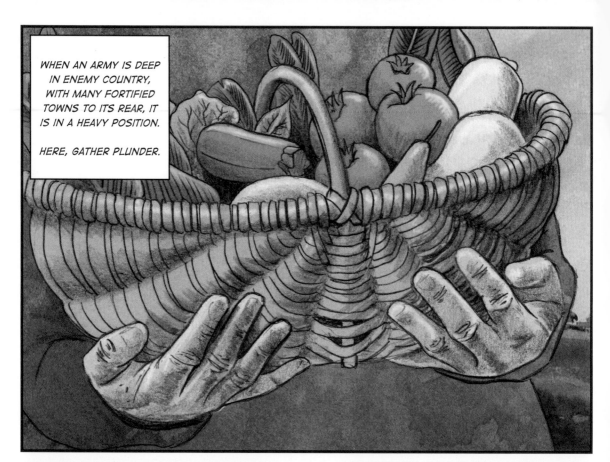

WHEN AN ARMY IS DEEP IN ENEMY COUNTRY, WITH MANY FORTIFIED TOWNS TO ITS REAR, IT IS IN A HEAVY POSITION.

HERE, GATHER PLUNDER.

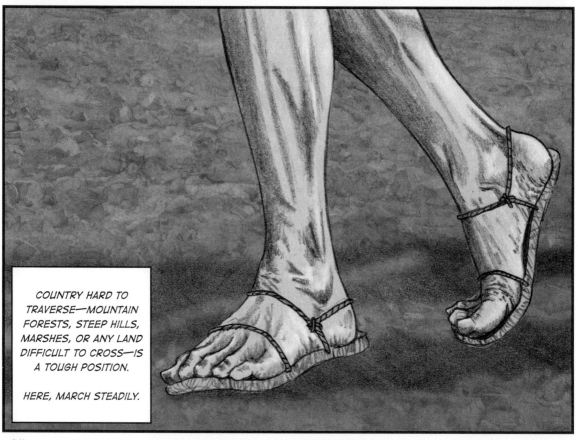

COUNTRY HARD TO TRAVERSE—MOUNTAIN FORESTS, STEEP HILLS, MARSHES, OR ANY LAND DIFFICULT TO CROSS—IS A TOUGH POSITION.

HERE, MARCH STEADILY.

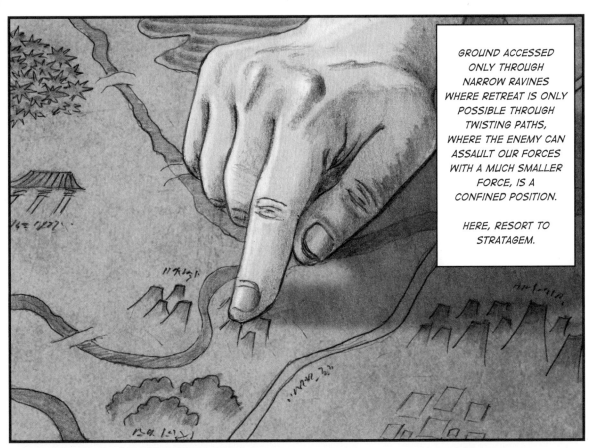

GROUND ACCESSED ONLY THROUGH NARROW RAVINES WHERE RETREAT IS ONLY POSSIBLE THROUGH TWISTING PATHS, WHERE THE ENEMY CAN ASSAULT OUR FORCES WITH A MUCH SMALLER FORCE, IS A CONFINED POSITION.

HERE, RESORT TO STRATAGEM.

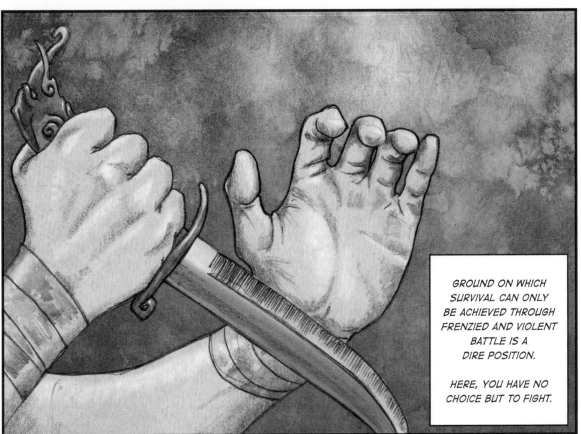

GROUND ON WHICH SURVIVAL CAN ONLY BE ACHIEVED THROUGH FRENZIED AND VIOLENT BATTLE IS A DIRE POSITION.

HERE, YOU HAVE NO CHOICE BUT TO FIGHT.

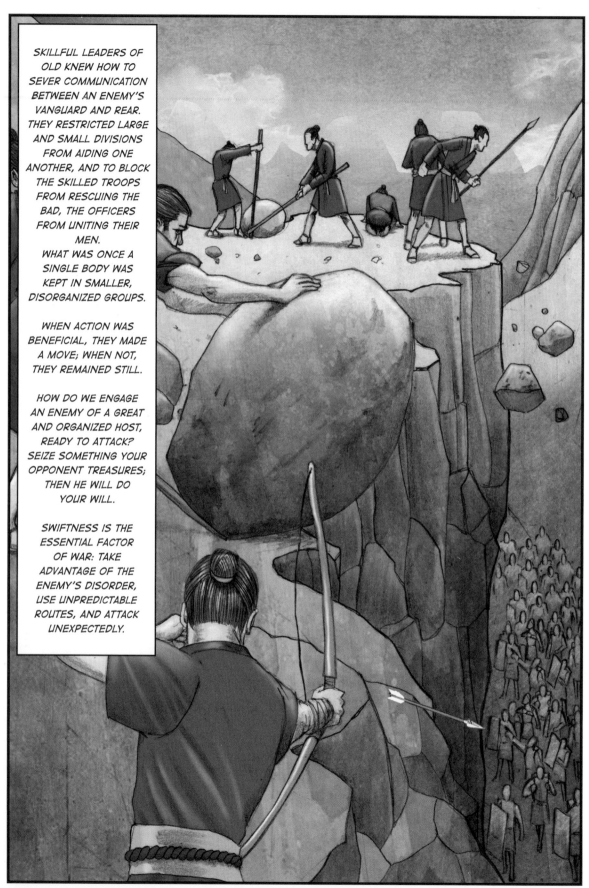

SKILLFUL LEADERS OF OLD KNEW HOW TO SEVER COMMUNICATION BETWEEN AN ENEMY'S VANGUARD AND REAR. THEY RESTRICTED LARGE AND SMALL DIVISIONS FROM AIDING ONE ANOTHER, AND TO BLOCK THE SKILLED TROOPS FROM RESCUING THE BAD, THE OFFICERS FROM UNITING THEIR MEN.
WHAT WAS ONCE A SINGLE BODY WAS KEPT IN SMALLER, DISORGANIZED GROUPS.

WHEN ACTION WAS BENEFICIAL, THEY MADE A MOVE; WHEN NOT, THEY REMAINED STILL.

HOW DO WE ENGAGE AN ENEMY OF A GREAT AND ORGANIZED HOST, READY TO ATTACK? SEIZE SOMETHING YOUR OPPONENT TREASURES; THEN HE WILL DO YOUR WILL.

SWIFTNESS IS THE ESSENTIAL FACTOR OF WAR: TAKE ADVANTAGE OF THE ENEMY'S DISORDER, USE UNPREDICTABLE ROUTES, AND ATTACK UNEXPECTEDLY.

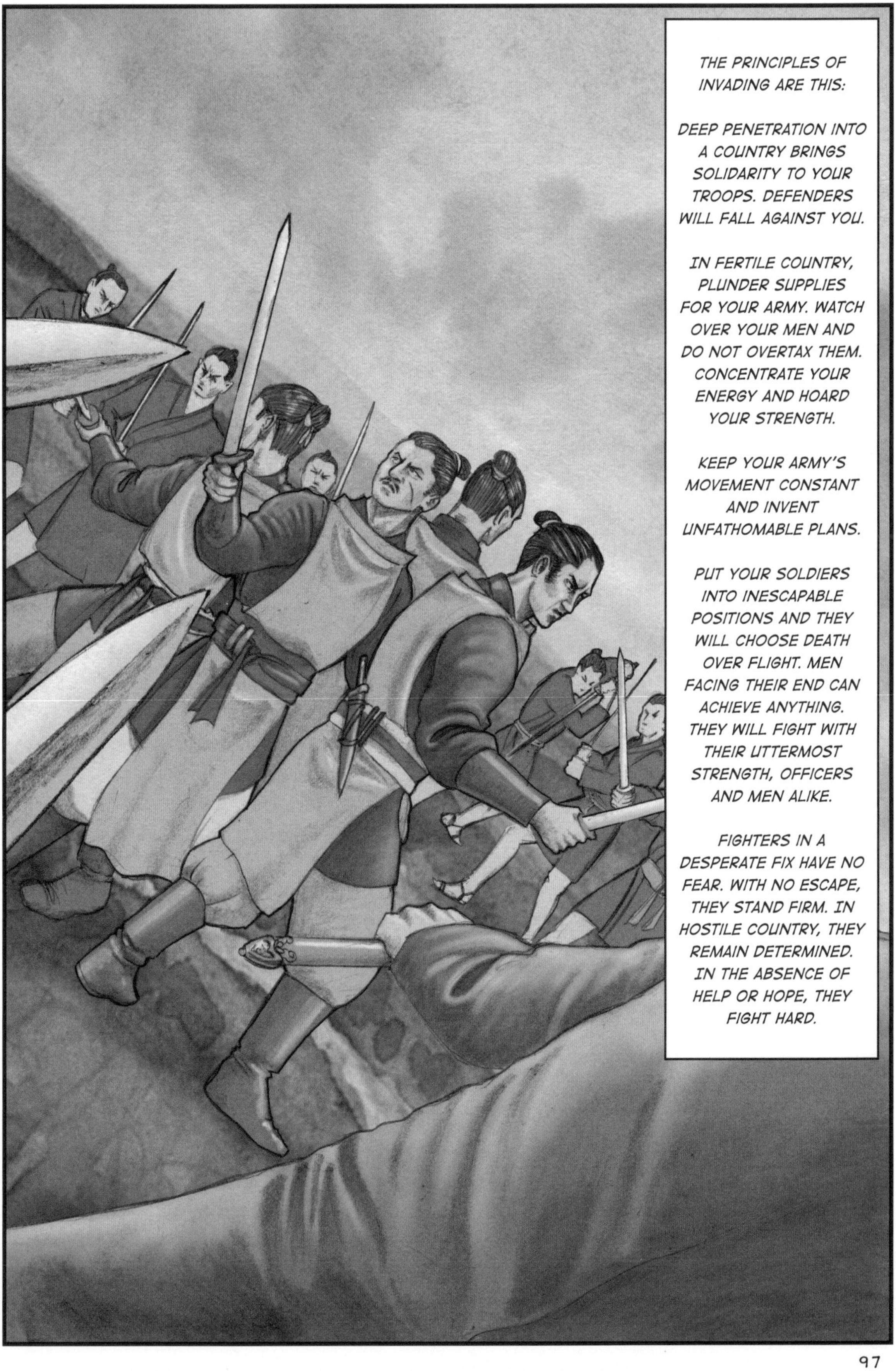
THE PRINCIPLES OF INVADING ARE THIS:
DEEP PENETRATION INTO A COUNTRY BRINGS SOLIDARITY TO YOUR TROOPS. DEFENDERS WILL FALL AGAINST YOU.
IN FERTILE COUNTRY, PLUNDER SUPPLIES FOR YOUR ARMY. WATCH OVER YOUR MEN AND DO NOT OVERTAX THEM. CONCENTRATE YOUR ENERGY AND HOARD YOUR STRENGTH.
KEEP YOUR ARMY'S MOVEMENT CONSTANT AND INVENT UNFATHOMABLE PLANS.
PUT YOUR SOLDIERS INTO INESCAPABLE POSITIONS AND THEY WILL CHOOSE DEATH OVER FLIGHT. MEN FACING THEIR END CAN ACHIEVE ANYTHING. THEY WILL FIGHT WITH THEIR UTTERMOST STRENGTH, OFFICERS AND MEN ALIKE.
FIGHTERS IN A DESPERATE FIX HAVE NO FEAR. WITH NO ESCAPE, THEY STAND FIRM. IN HOSTILE COUNTRY, THEY REMAIN DETERMINED. IN THE ABSENCE OF HELP OR HOPE, THEY FIGHT HARD.

THEY KEEP SHARP WITH NO NEED OF DISCIPLINE, THEY PERFORM THEIR DUTIES WITH NO NEED OF INSTRUCTION, THEY WILL BE FAITHFUL WITHOUT RESTRICTIONS AND CAN BE TRUSTED WITHOUT COMMAND.

FORBID THE READING OF OMENS TO ELIMINATE SUPERSTITIOUS DOUBTS. THEN THE MEN WILL JOIN YOU UNTIL DEATH.

OUR SOLDIERS ARE NOT RICH, BUT NOT BECAUSE THEY DISLIKE RICHES. IF THEIR LIVES ARE CUT SHORT, IT IS NOT BECAUSE THEY ARE ADVERSE TO LONG LIFE.

WHAT MASTER TZU MEANS HERE IS THAT WEALTH AND LONG LIFE ARE WHAT MOST MEN DESIRE.

SO IF THEY BURN THEIR VALUABLES AND SACRIFICE THEIR LIVES, IT IS NOT THAT THEY DON'T WANT THEM, BUT SIMPLY THEY HAVE NO CHOICE AND WILL DO WHAT THEY MUST.

ON THE DAY THEY ARE SENT OUT TO BATTLE, YOUR SOLDIERS MAY WEEP, WETTING THEIR CHEEKS WITH TEARS. BUT SEND THEM TO AN INESCAPABLE PLACE, AND THEY WILL DISPLAY THE COURAGE OF HEROES OF OLD.

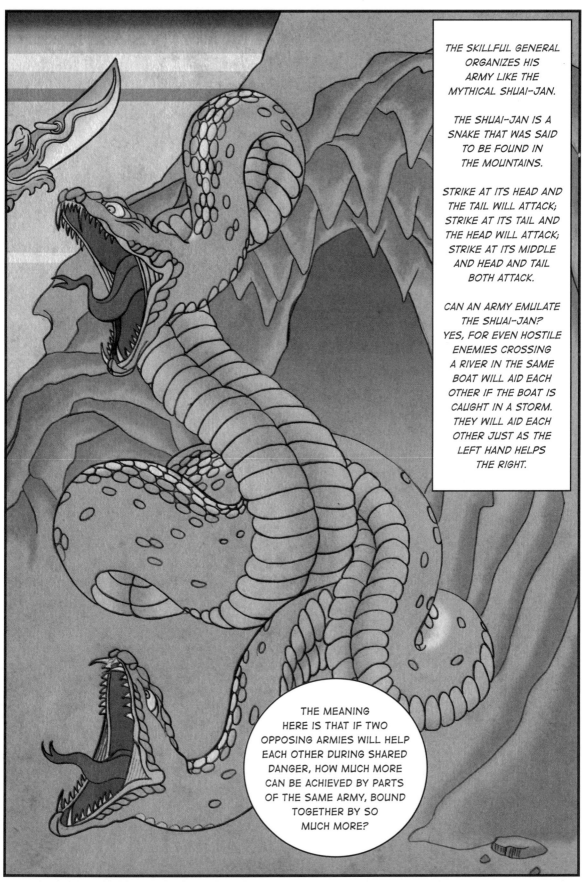

THE SKILLFUL GENERAL ORGANIZES HIS ARMY LIKE THE MYTHICAL SHUAI-JAN.

THE SHUAI-JAN IS A SNAKE THAT WAS SAID TO BE FOUND IN THE MOUNTAINS.

STRIKE AT ITS HEAD AND THE TAIL WILL ATTACK; STRIKE AT ITS TAIL AND THE HEAD WILL ATTACK; STRIKE AT ITS MIDDLE AND HEAD AND TAIL BOTH ATTACK.

CAN AN ARMY EMULATE THE SHUAI-JAN? YES, FOR EVEN HOSTILE ENEMIES CROSSING A RIVER IN THE SAME BOAT WILL AID EACH OTHER IF THE BOAT IS CAUGHT IN A STORM. THEY WILL AID EACH OTHER JUST AS THE LEFT HAND HELPS THE RIGHT.

THE MEANING HERE IS THAT IF TWO OPPOSING ARMIES WILL HELP EACH OTHER DURING SHARED DANGER, HOW MUCH MORE CAN BE ACHIEVED BY PARTS OF THE SAME ARMY, BOUND TOGETHER BY SO MUCH MORE?

IT IS NOT ENOUGH TO TETHER HORSES AND BURY CHARIOT WHEELS IN THE GROUND TO PREVENT YOUR ARMY FROM FLEEING.

UNITE YOUR MEN TO A SINGLE STANDARD OF COURAGE. THIS IS HOW TO MANAGE AN ARMY.

WITH PROPER USE OF THE GROUND, ALL MEN CAN USEFULLY SERVE, BOTH STRONG AND WEAK.

THE SKILLFUL GENERAL CONDUCTS HIS ARMY JUST AS THOUGH IT WERE A SINGLE MAN, WITH NO ROOM FOR CONFUSION.

IT IS THE BUSINESS OF A GENERAL TO BE CALM AND TACITURN, ENSURING SECRECY; UPRIGHT AND FAIR, ENSURING ORDER.

WITH FALSE REPORTS
AND APPEARANCES, HE
KEEPS HIS OFFICERS
AND MEN
IN IGNORANCE.

BY CHANGING
ARRANGEMENTS AND
PLANS, BY SHIFTING
CAMP OR TAKING
DIVERGENT ROUTES, HE
KEEPS THE ENEMY
IN IGNORANCE.

HE DRIVES HIS MEN THIS
WAY AND THAT, SO
NO ONE CAN GUESS
HIS DESTINATION.

AT THE CRITICAL
MOMENT, THE LEADER
OF AN ARMY ACTS LIKE
ONE WHO HAS CLIMBED
HIGH THEN KICKS AWAY
THE LADDER.
HE LEADS HIS MEN
DEEP INTO HOSTILE
TERRITORY BEFORE
REVEALING HIS PLANS.
HE BURNS HIS BOATS
AND BREAKS HIS
COOKING POTS.
HE GATHERS HIS HOST
AND BRINGS IT
INTO DANGER.

THIS IS THE BUSINESS
OF THE GENERAL.

THESE THINGS MUST BE CAREFULLY STUDIED: THE PRINCIPLES OF THE NINE TYPES OF POSITION, THE APPLICABLE TACTICS, AND THE FUNDAMENTAL LAWS OF HUMAN NATURE.

WHEN INVADING HOSTILE TERRITORY, THE GENERAL PRINCIPLE IS THAT PENETRATING DEEPLY BRINGS UNITY. PENETRATING ONLY A SHORT DISTANCE INVITES DISPERSION.

WHEN YOU LEAVE YOUR OWN LAND AND TRAVEL WITH YOUR TROOPS ACROSS NEIGHBORING TERRITORY, YOU FIND YOURSELF IN AN ISOLATED POSITION.

WHEN THERE ARE MEANS OF COMMUNICATION IN EVERY DIRECTION, YOU ARE IN AN INTERSECTING POSITION.

WHEN YOU PENETRATE DEEPLY INTO A COUNTRY, IT IS A HEAVY POSITION. WHEN YOU PENETRATE BUT A SHORT WAY, IT IS A SIMPLE POSITION.

WHEN YOU HAVE THE ENEMY'S STRONGHOLDS TO YOUR REAR AND NARROW PASSES IN FRONT, IT IS A CONFINED POSITION.

WHEN THERE IS NO RESPITE OF SANCTUARY AT ALL, IT IS A DIRE POSITION.

SO, ON SCATTERING GROUND, UNIFY YOUR MEN TO A SINGLE PURPOSE.

ON SIMPLE GROUND, SEE YOUR ARMY IS WELL-CONNECTED.

ON CONTENTIOUS GROUND, BRING UP YOUR REAR.

ON OPEN GROUND, SECURE YOUR DEFENSES.

ON INTERSECTING GROUND, BOLSTER YOUR ALLIANCES.

ON HEAVY GROUND, ENSURE SUPPLIES ARE CONTINUOUS.

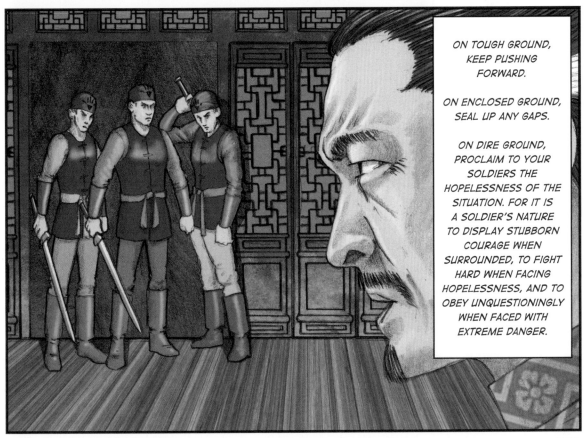

ON TOUGH GROUND, KEEP PUSHING FORWARD.

ON ENCLOSED GROUND, SEAL UP ANY GAPS.

ON DIRE GROUND, PROCLAIM TO YOUR SOLDIERS THE HOPELESSNESS OF THE SITUATION. FOR IT IS A SOLDIER'S NATURE TO DISPLAY STUBBORN COURAGE WHEN SURROUNDED, TO FIGHT HARD WHEN FACING HOPELESSNESS, AND TO OBEY UNQUESTIONINGLY WHEN FACED WITH EXTREME DANGER.

WE CANNOT MAKE ASTUTE ALLIANCES WITHOUT KNOWLEDGE OF A POTENTIAL ALLY'S OR ADVERSARY'S DESIGNS.

WITHOUT HAVING INTIMATE KNOWLEDGE OF OUR SURROUNDINGS—THE MOUNTAINS AND FORESTS, PITFALLS AND PRECIPICES, MARSHES AND SWAMPS—WE CANNOT MARCH.

WE CANNOT UTILIZE THE ADVANTAGES OF OUR SURROUNDINGS WITHOUT THE USE OF LOCAL GUIDES.

IGNORANCE OF ANY OF THESE PRINCIPLES DOES NOT BEFIT A RESPONSIBLE GENERAL.

WHEN A GREAT RULER'S ARMY ATTACKS A GREAT STATE, HE PREVENTS THE CONCENTRATION OF THE ENEMY'S FORCES. HE OVERWHELMS HIS OPPONENTS, PREVENTING THEM FROM FORMING ANY ALLIANCES. HE DOES NOT STRIVE FOR ALLIANCES WITH OTHER STATES, HE DOESN'T FOSTER THEIR POWER. HE EXTENDS HIS OWN INFLUENCE, CARRIES OUT HIS OWN DESIGNS, KEEPING HIS ENEMIES IN AWE. THUS, HE IS ABLE TO CAPTURE THEIR CITIES AND OVERTHROW THEIR STATE.

BESTOW INCREDIBLE REWARDS, ISSUE SURPRISING COMMANDS, AND YOU WILL BE ABLE TO MANAGE A WHOLE ARMY AS THOUGH IT WERE A SINGLE MAN.

SET YOUR SOLDIERS TO THEIR TASKS WITHOUT UNNECESSARY DETAILS. THEY NEED NOT KNOW THE GAIN, BUT REVEAL THE DANGERS WHEN THE SITUATION IS DIRE.

PLACE YOUR MEN IN GRAVE DANGER AND THEY WILL SURVIVE; PLUNGE THEM INTO INESCAPABLE SITUATIONS AND THEY WILL LIBERATE THEMSELVES TO SAFETY.

FOR IT IS PRECISELY WHEN A SOLDIER FALLS INTO CRISIS THAT HE IS PRONE TO FANTASTIC FEATS OF VICTORY.

SUCCESS IN WAGING
WAR COMES WITH
CAREFUL SCRUTINY OF
THE ENEMY'S PLANS.
IT IS GAINED BY
SEEMING TO OBLIGE
THE ENEMY IN
THEIR PURPOSE.

BY CONCENTRATING
SOLELY ON THE ENEMY
WITH ALL YOUR WILL
AND STRENGTH, YOU
WILL BE ABLE TO SLAY
THE ENEMY GENERAL
FROM EVEN A
GREAT DISTANCE.

THIS IS HOW TO
ACCOMPLISH YOUR
GOALS WITH
SHEER CUNNING.

ON THE DAY THAT YOU TAKE UP YOUR COMMAND AND WAR IS DECLARED, BLOCK THE BORDER PASSES, DESTROY ALL TRAVEL PERMITS, AND STOP ANY CONTACT WITH ALL ENEMY EMISSARIES.

BE STERN IN THE COUNCIL CHAMBER, SO THAT YOUR CONTROL IS UNQUESTIONED.

IF THE ENEMY PROVIDES AN OPENING, YOU MUST RUSH TO TAKE ADVANTAGE OF IT. SEIZE WHAT HE HOLDS DEAR, SO HE IS MANIPULATED TO A BATTLE OF YOUR CHOOSING.

SCRUTINIZE THE ENEMY, REVISING YOUR PLANS UNTIL YOU CAN FIGHT THE DECISIVE BATTLE.

AT FIRST, BE COY AS A MAIDEN, UNTIL THE ENEMY PRESENTS AN OPENING; THEN BE SWIFT AS A HARE, AND IT WILL BE TOO LATE FOR THEM TO OPPOSE YOU.

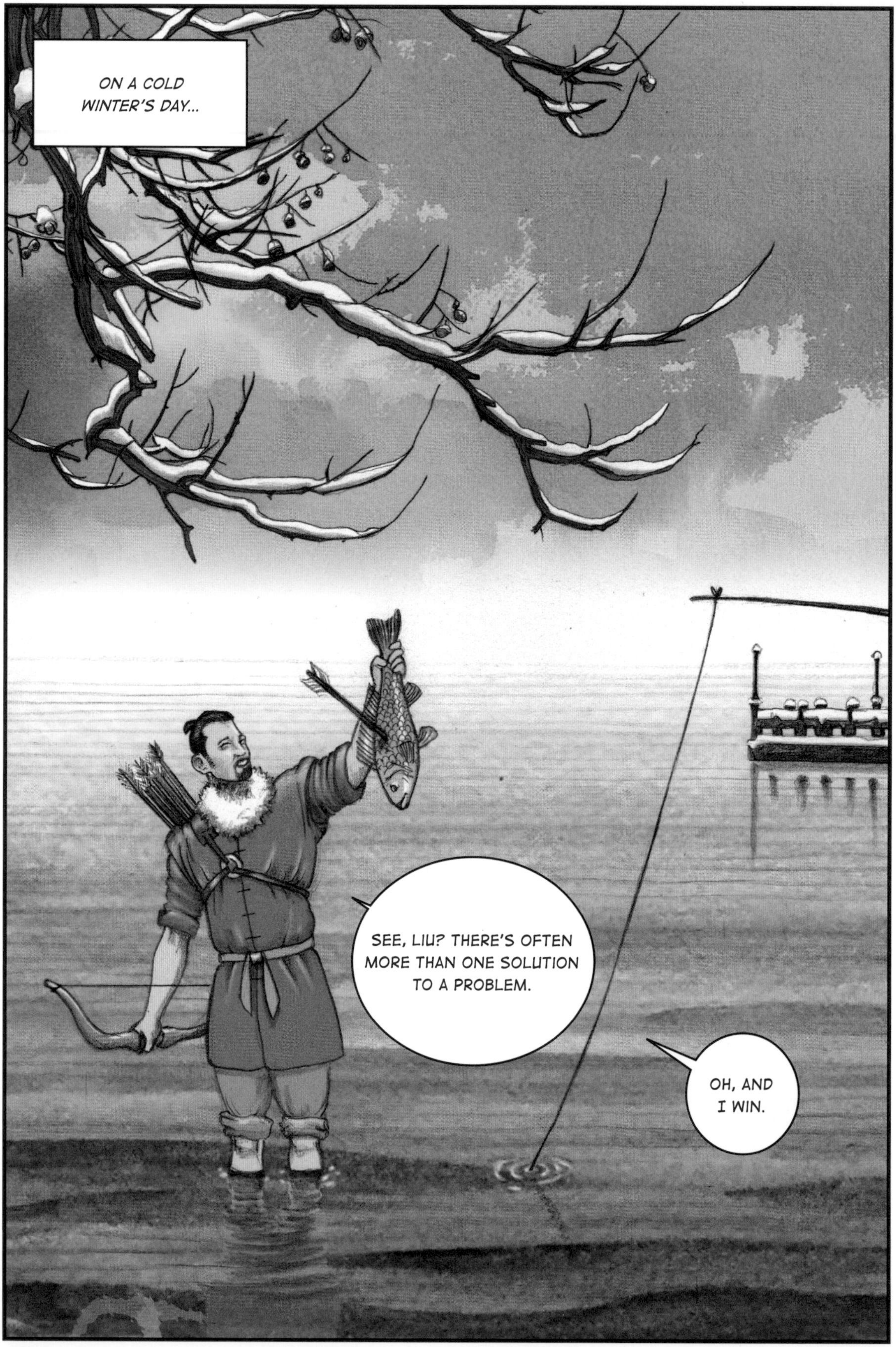
ON A COLD WINTER'S DAY...
SEE, LIU? THERE'S OFTEN MORE THAN ONE SOLUTION TO A PROBLEM.
OH, AND I WIN.

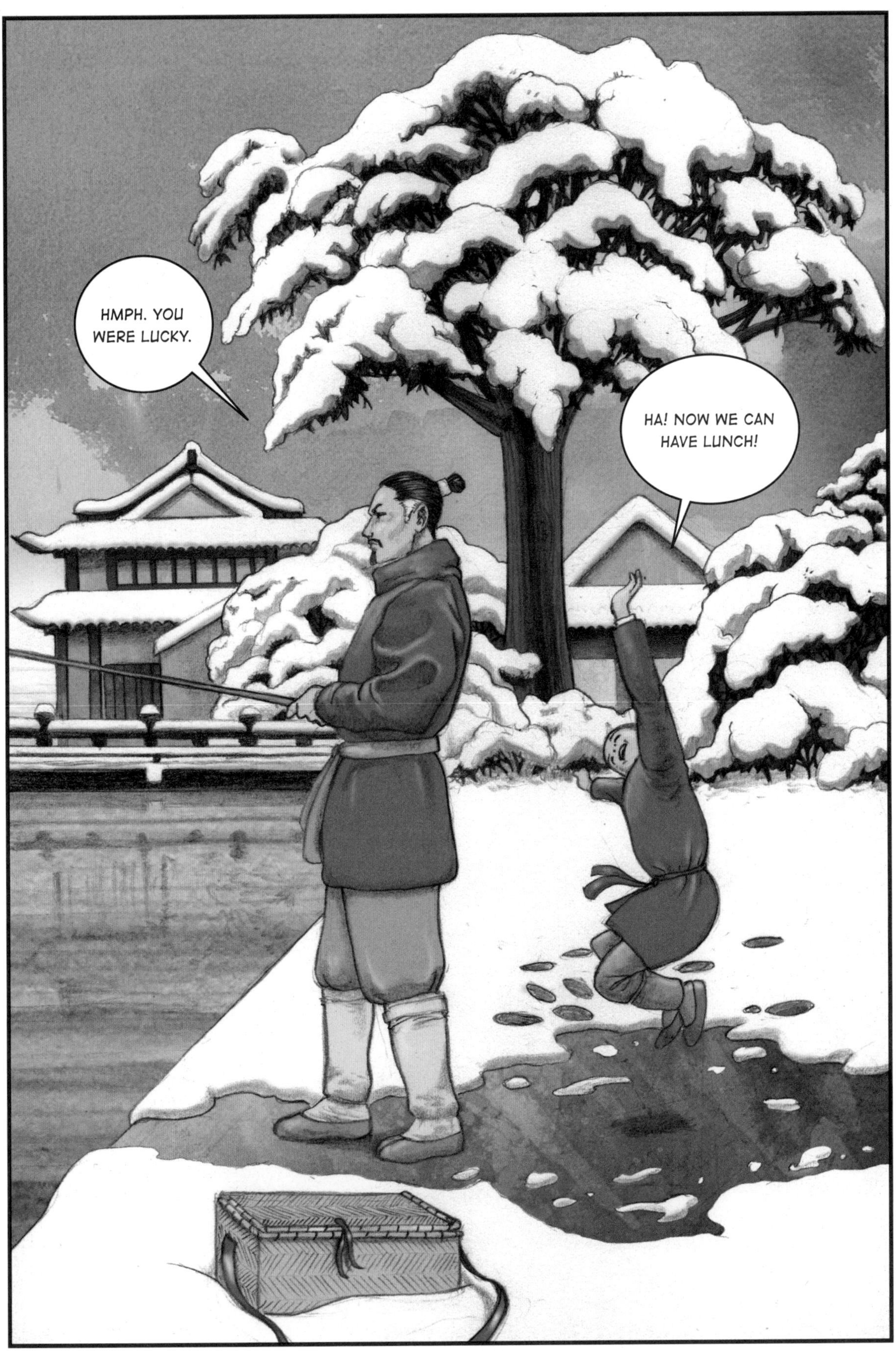
HMPH. YOU WERE LUCKY.
HA! NOW WE CAN HAVE LUNCH!

PART TWELVE

ATTACK BY FIRE

SUN TZU SAID: *THERE ARE FIVE WAYS TO ATTACK WITH FIRE.*

THE FIRST IS TO BURN SOLDIERS IN CAMP. THE SECOND IS TO BURN STORES.

THE THIRD IS BURNING SUPPLY TRAINS.

THE FOURTH IS TO BURN WEAPONS AND EQUIPMENT.

THE FIFTH IS TO HURL FIRE THROUGH THE SKY.

IN ORDER TO CARRY OUT SUCH AN ATTACK, WE MUST HAVE THE MEANS AND MATERIALS AVAILABLE AND AT THE READY.

HE IS ALSO REFERRING TO THE NECESSITY OF SPIES OR TRAITORS PLACED IN THE ENEMY CAMP WHO, AT THE RIGHT MOMENT, START FIRES AMONG THE TENTS.

MASTER TZU ISN'T JUST REFERRING TO ARROWS, OIL, AND KINDLING HERE.

THERE IS A PROPER SEASON AND THERE ARE SPECIAL DAYS FOR MAKING AN ATTACK WITH FIRE.

THE PROPER SEASON IS WHEN THE WEATHER IS HOT AND DRY.

THE SPECIAL DAYS FALL WHEN THE MOON IS IN THE CONSTELLATIONS OF SAGITTARIUS, PEGASUS, CRATER, AND CORVUS—FOR THESE ARE ALL DAYS OF RISING WIND.

WHEN ATTACKING WITH FIRE, BE PREPARED FOR THESE POSSIBLE DEVELOPMENTS:

WHEN FIRE BREAKS OUT WITHIN THE ENEMY CAMP, ATTACK AT ONCE FROM WITHOUT.

IF FIRE BREAKS OUT BUT THE ENEMY REMAINS CALM, HOLD BACK AND DO NOT ATTACK. WHEN THE FORCE OF THE FLAMES HAVE REACHED THEIR PEAK, FOLLOW UP WITH YOUR ATTACK IF PRACTICAL; IF NOT, KEEP YOUR POSITION.

IF A FIRE ATTACK IS POSSIBLE FROM OUTSIDE A CAMP, DO NOT WAIT FOR IT TO BE STARTED INSIDE. ATTACK WHEN THE TIME IS RIGHT.

WHEN STARTING A FIRE, BE UPWIND; NEVER START A FIRE ATTACK DOWNWIND.

A WIND IN THE DAY LASTS LONG, BUT A NIGHTTIME BREEZE SOON FAILS.

WHEN PLANNING TO USE FIRE, KEEP IN MIND THESE DEVELOPMENTS; WATCH THE STARS AND KEEP NOTE OF THE PROPER DAYS.

I SUPPOSE KNOWING THE DAYS OF RISING WIND MUST BE IMPORTANT FOR ALL GENERALS, SIFU.

ON THOSE DAYS, EVEN IF YOU DON'T PLAN ON USING FIRE, YOUR ENEMY IS MORE LIKELY TO. I WOULD SET EXTRA WATCHES ON THOSE DAYS.

YOU, YOUNG MAN, SHOW PROMISE OF BECOMING A FORMIDABLE GENERAL.

USING FIRE PROPERLY ADDS A TOOL OF INTELLECT. USING WATER PROPERLY ADDS A TOOL OF STRENGTH.

BY MEANS OF WATER AN ENEMY MAY BE HINDERED OR DIVIDED, BUT WATER LACKS THE DESTRUCTIVE POWER OF FIRE.

BLOCKING, SLOWING, OR DIVIDING AN ENEMY CAN BE DONE WITH WATER, BUT IT WON'T CAUSE OUTRIGHT DESTRUCTION...

...UNLESS YOUR ENEMY WAS STUPID ENOUGH TO CAMP BELOW A DAM!

TO ENSURE SUCCESS IN BATTLE, DO NOT SIMPLY SIT STILL AND HOLD TO YOUR ADVANTAGE; STRIKE AT THE RIGHT TIME WITH FIRE, WATER, OR ANY MEASURES AT YOUR DISPOSAL.

THE ENLIGHTENED RULER PLANS METICULOUSLY, THE EFFECTIVE GENERAL MOVES DECISIVELY.

MOVE ONLY FOR AN ADVANTAGE, USE YOUR TROOPS ONLY FOR GAIN, FIGHT ONLY WHEN THE POSITION IS CRITICAL.

NO RULER SHOULD SEND TROOPS OUT OF WRATH, NO GENERAL SHOULD FIGHT A BATTLE OUT OF VEXATION.

IF IT IS TO YOUR ADVANTAGE, MAKE YOUR MOVE; IF NOT, STAY WHERE YOU ARE.

ANGER MAY IN TIME CHANGE TO GLADNESS; VEXATION MAY TURN TO CONTENT. BUT A KINGDOM ONCE DESTROYED CAN NEVER BE REBUILT, NOR A DEAD MAN BROUGHT BACK TO LIFE.

THE ENLIGHTENED RULER IS HEEDFUL, AND THE EFFECTIVE GENERAL FULL OF CAUTION. THIS IS THE WAY TO KEEP A COUNTRY AT PEACE AND AN ARMY INTACT.

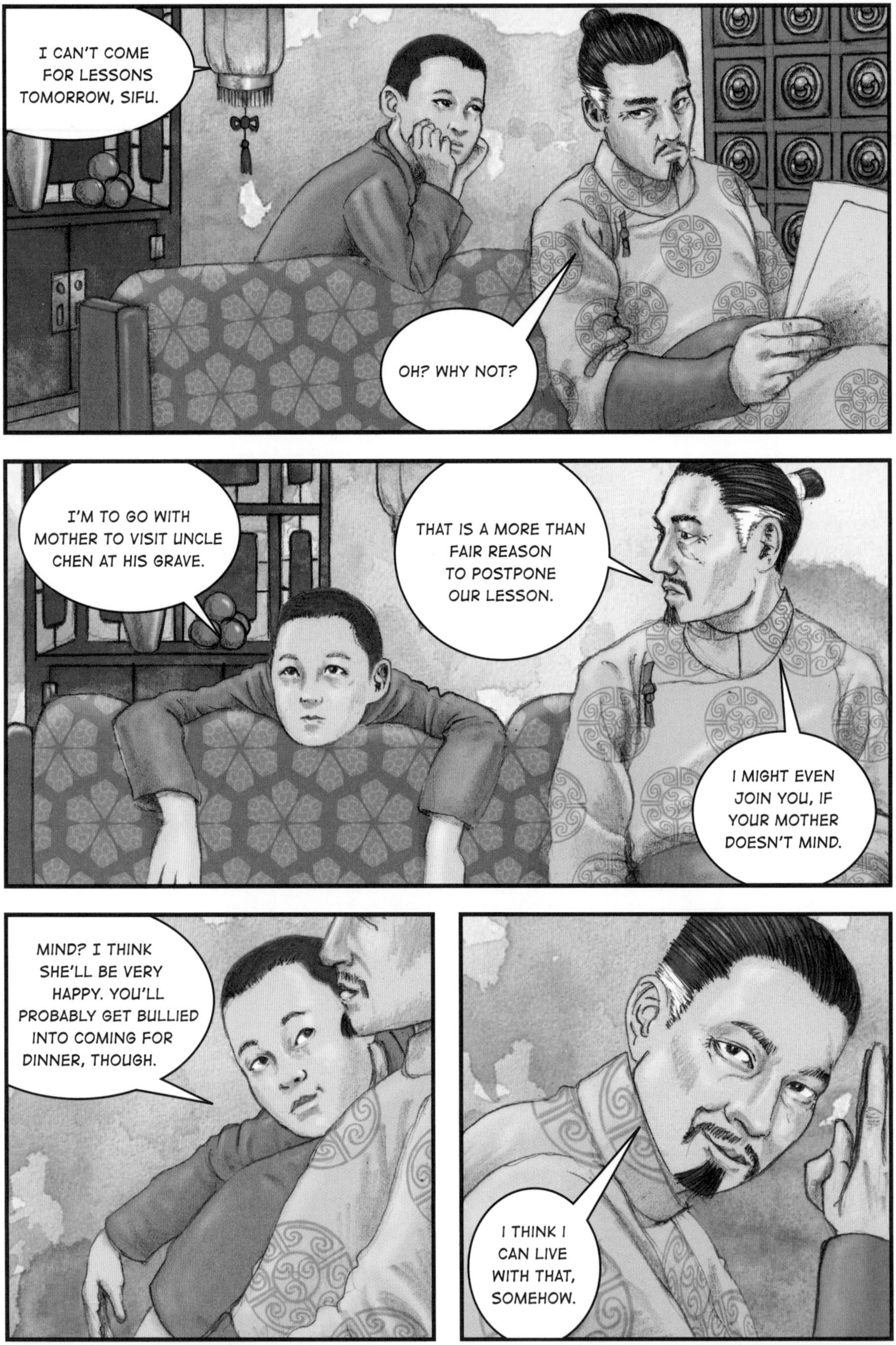
I CAN'T COME FOR LESSONS TOMORROW, SIFU.
OH? WHY NOT?
I'M TO GO WITH MOTHER TO VISIT UNCLE CHEN AT HIS GRAVE.
THAT IS A MORE THAN FAIR REASON TO POSTPONE OUR LESSON.
I MIGHT EVEN JOIN YOU, IF YOUR MOTHER DOESN'T MIND.
MIND? I THINK SHE'LL BE VERY HAPPY. YOU'LL PROBABLY GET BULLIED INTO COMING FOR DINNER, THOUGH.
I THINK I CAN LIVE WITH THAT, SOMEHOW.

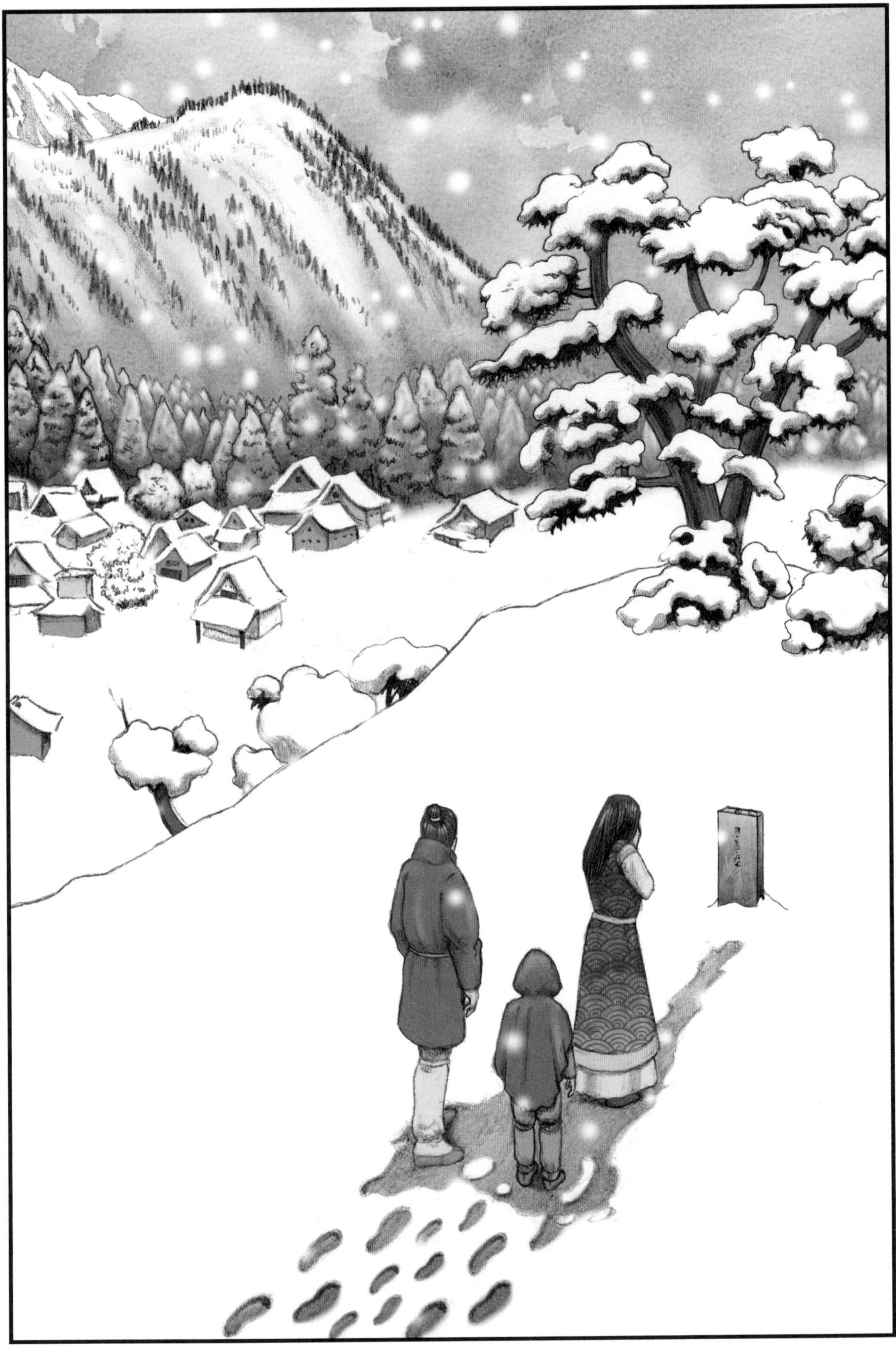

PART THIRTEEN

SPIES

SUN TZU SAID: RAISING AN ARMY OF A HUNDRED THOUSAND MEN AND MARCHING THEM GREAT DISTANCES BRINGS HEAVY LOSS TO THE PEOPLE AND DRAINS THE STATE, TO THE DAILY SUM OF A THOUSAND OUNCES OF SILVER. IT BRINGS COMMOTION AT HOME AND ABROAD, AND LEAVES MEN DROPPING EXHAUSTED ALONG THE ROADS. IT KEEPS SEVEN HUNDRED THOUSAND FAMILIES FROM THEIR NORMAL WORK. A GREAT WORRY INDEED.

HOSTILE ARMIES MAY FACE EACH OTHER FOR YEARS, STRIVING FOR A SINGLE DECISIVE VICTORY.

TO KNOW THIS, BUT TO REMAIN WILLINGLY IGNORANT OF THE ENEMY'S CONDITION SIMPLY BECAUSE ONE BEGRUDGES THE OUTLAY OF A HUNDRED OUNCES OF SILVER FOR KNOWLEDGE, IS THE HEIGHT OF INHUMANITY AND LUNACY.

A PENNY-PINCHER SUCH AS THIS IS NO LEADER OF MEN, NO HELP TO HIS SOVEREIGN, NO MASTER OF VICTORY.

WHAT ENABLES THE WISE SOVEREIGN AND THE CAPABLE GENERAL TO STRIKE, CONQUER, AND ACHIEVE THINGS BEYOND THE REACH OF ORDINARY MEN IS FOREKNOWLEDGE.

THIS FOREKNOWLEDGE CANNOT BE ELICITED FROM SPIRITS; IT CANNOT BE OBTAINED THROUGH EXPERIENCE, NOR BY ANY CALCULATION.

FOREKNOWLEDGE OF THE ENEMY'S PLANS AND DISPOSITIONS CAN ONLY BE OBTAINED FROM OTHER MEN.

FROM SPIES.

THERE ARE FIVE CLASSES OF SPY: LOCAL SPIES, INNER SPIES, DUAL SPIES, DOOMED SPIES, AND ENDURING SPIES.

WHEN THESE FIVE KINDS OF SPY ARE ALL IN PLAY, NONE CAN GUESS THEIR PURPOSE. THIS IS CALLED THE UNSEEN WEB. IT IS A RULER'S GREATEST TREASURE.

LOCAL SPIES ARE EMPLOYED FROM THE COMMON INHABITANTS OF AN ENEMY'S DISTRICT.

INNER SPIES ARE OFFICIALS OF THE ENEMY.

ENEMY SPIES THAT NOW WORK FOR YOUR CAUSE ARE DUAL SPIES.

DOOMED SPIES CARRY DELIBERATELY FALSE INFORMATION TO THE ENEMY.

ENDURING SPIES ARE THOSE WHO SUCCESSFULLY BRING BACK INFORMATION FROM THE ENEMY.

INNER SPIES COULD BE ONCE-WORTHY MEN, DEMOTED FROM OFFICE; FAVORITE CONCUBINES, GREEDY FOR RICHES; PUNISHED CRIMINALS; OR AMBITIOUS MEN IN SUBORDINATE POSITIONS.

A DOOMED SPY DOES NOT KNOW HE IS DOOMED. HE RELAYS WHAT HE THINKS IS CORRECT INFORMATION TO THE ENEMY, WHO REACTS ACCORDINGLY.

ONCE IT IS CLEAR THE INFORMATION WAS FALSE, THE SPY IS UNDOUBTEDLY PUT TO DEATH.

NO SOLDIER IS CLOSER TO A LEADER IN THE WHOLE ARMY THAN HIS SPIES. NONE SHOULD BE MORE LIBERALLY REWARDED.

IN NO OTHER BUSINESS SHOULD GREATER SECRECY BE PRESERVED.

SPIES CANNOT BE USEFULLY EMPLOYED WITHOUT MUCH SAGACITY.

THEY CANNOT BE PROPERLY MANAGED WITHOUT GENEROSITY AND DIRECTNESS.

WITHOUT SUBTLE INGENUITY OF MIND, ONE CANNOT MAKE CERTAIN THE TRUTH OF THEIR REPORTS.

IF SECRET INFORMATION IS LEAKED BY A SPY TOO EARLY, BOTH HE AND THE RECIPIENT MUST BE KILLED.

BE SUBTLE AND USE YOUR SPIES FOR MANY SITUATIONS, AS THEIR USE IS LIMITLESS.

SPIES ARE MASTERS OF DECEPTION, BUT YOU MUST SEE THROUGH THEM, OTHERWISE YOU MAY NOT RECOGNIZE A ONCE FAITHFUL BUT NOW TRAITOROUS SPY IN YOUR MIDST.

WHETHER CRUSHING AN ARMY, STORMING A CITY, OR ASSASSINATING AN INDIVIDUAL, IT IS ALWAYS NECESSARY TO FIRST KNOW THE NAMES OF THE ATTENDANTS, THE AIDES, THE SENTRIES, AND THE GENERAL IN COMMAND.

OUR SPIES MUST BE COMMISSIONED TO DISCOVER THESE.

ENEMY SPIES WHO COME TO SPY ON US MUST BE SOUGHT OUT, BRIBED, WELL TREATED, AND COMFORTABLY HOUSED. THEY WILL BECOME DUAL SPIES FOR OUR CAUSE.

THROUGH THE INFORMATION BROUGHT BY THE DUAL SPY, WE ARE ABLE TO FIND AND EMPLOY LOCAL AND INNER SPIES.

THE DUAL SPY INFORMS US HOW BEST TO RELAY FALSE INFORMATION TO THE ENEMY USING DOOMED SPIES.

THE DUAL SPY INFORMS US OF THE MOST OPPORTUNE OCCASIONS TO USE SURVIVING SPIES.

KNOWLEDGE OF THE ENEMY IS THE AIM OF ALL FIVE KINDS OF SPYING, AND THIS KNOWLEDGE CAN ONLY BE DERIVED, IN THE FIRST INSTANCE, FROM THE DUAL SPY.

HENCE IT IS ESSENTIAL TO TREAT THE DUAL SPY WITH THE UTMOST GENEROSITY.

ONLY THE ENLIGHTENED RULER AND WISE GENERAL CAN USE THE HIGHEST INTELLIGENCE FOR SPYING, AND THEREBY ACHIEVE GREAT RESULTS.

INTELLIGENCE IS A MOST IMPORTANT ELEMENT IN WAR, BECAUSE ON IT, EVERY ARMY'S ACTIONS DEPEND.

A WORD OF WARNING. WATER USEFULLY CARRIES A BOAT FROM BANK TO BANK, BUT MAY ALSO CAUSE IT TO SINK.

RELIANCE ON SPIES BRINGS GREAT RESULTS, BUT CAN ALSO BE THE SOURCE OF UTTER DESTRUCTION.

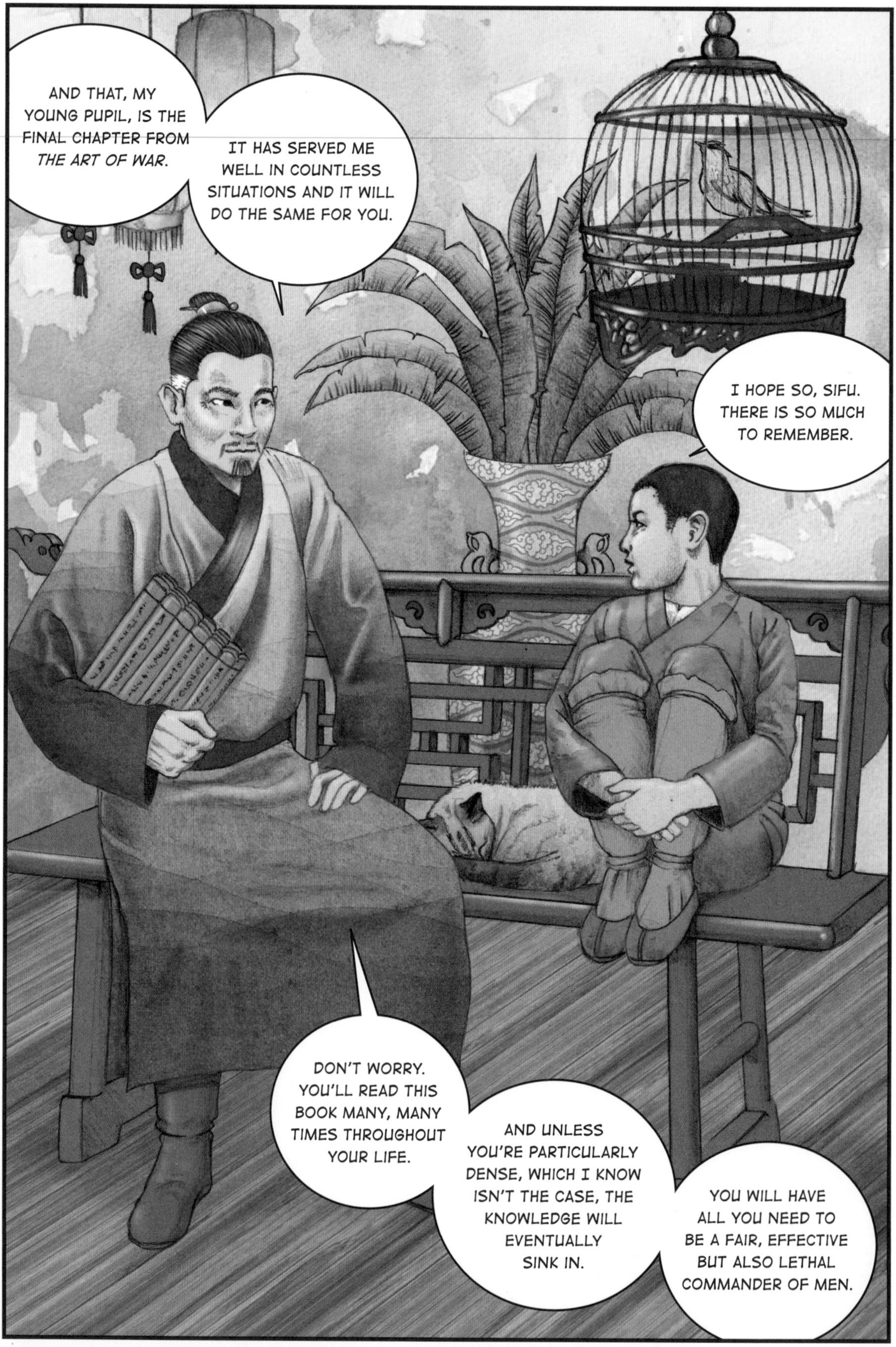
AND THAT, MY YOUNG PUPIL, IS THE FINAL CHAPTER FROM *THE ART OF WAR*.
IT HAS SERVED ME WELL IN COUNTLESS SITUATIONS AND IT WILL DO THE SAME FOR YOU.
I HOPE SO, SIFU. THERE IS SO MUCH TO REMEMBER.
DON'T WORRY. YOU'LL READ THIS BOOK MANY, MANY TIMES THROUGHOUT YOUR LIFE.
AND UNLESS YOU'RE PARTICULARLY DENSE, WHICH I KNOW ISN'T THE CASE, THE KNOWLEDGE WILL EVENTUALLY SINK IN.
YOU WILL HAVE ALL YOU NEED TO BE A FAIR, EFFECTIVE BUT ALSO LETHAL COMMANDER OF MEN.

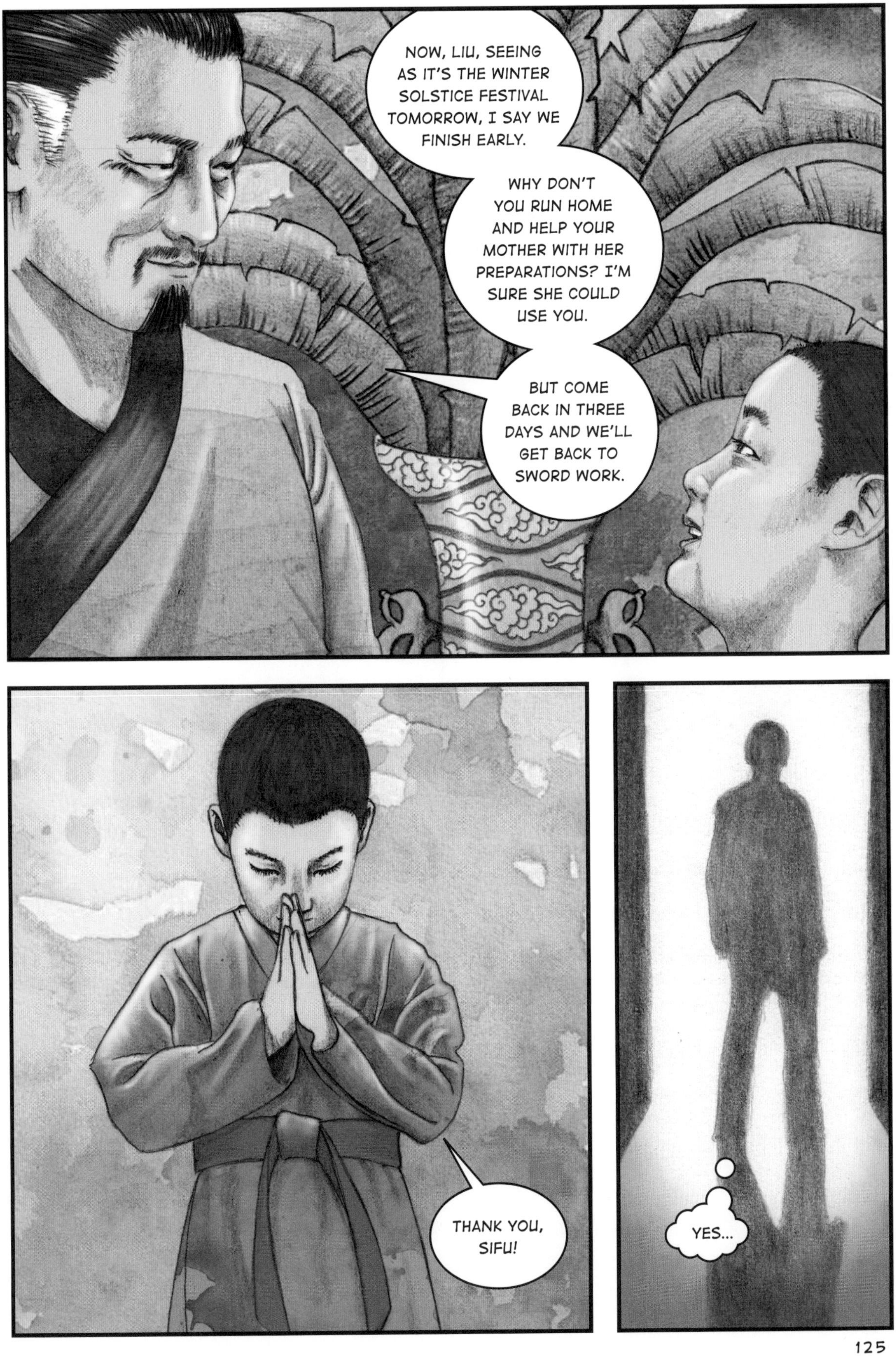
NOW, LIU, SEEING AS IT'S THE WINTER SOLSTICE FESTIVAL TOMORROW, I SAY WE FINISH EARLY.
WHY DON'T YOU RUN HOME AND HELP YOUR MOTHER WITH HER PREPARATIONS? I'M SURE SHE COULD USE YOU.
BUT COME BACK IN THREE DAYS AND WE'LL GET BACK TO SWORD WORK.
THANK YOU, SIFU!
YES...

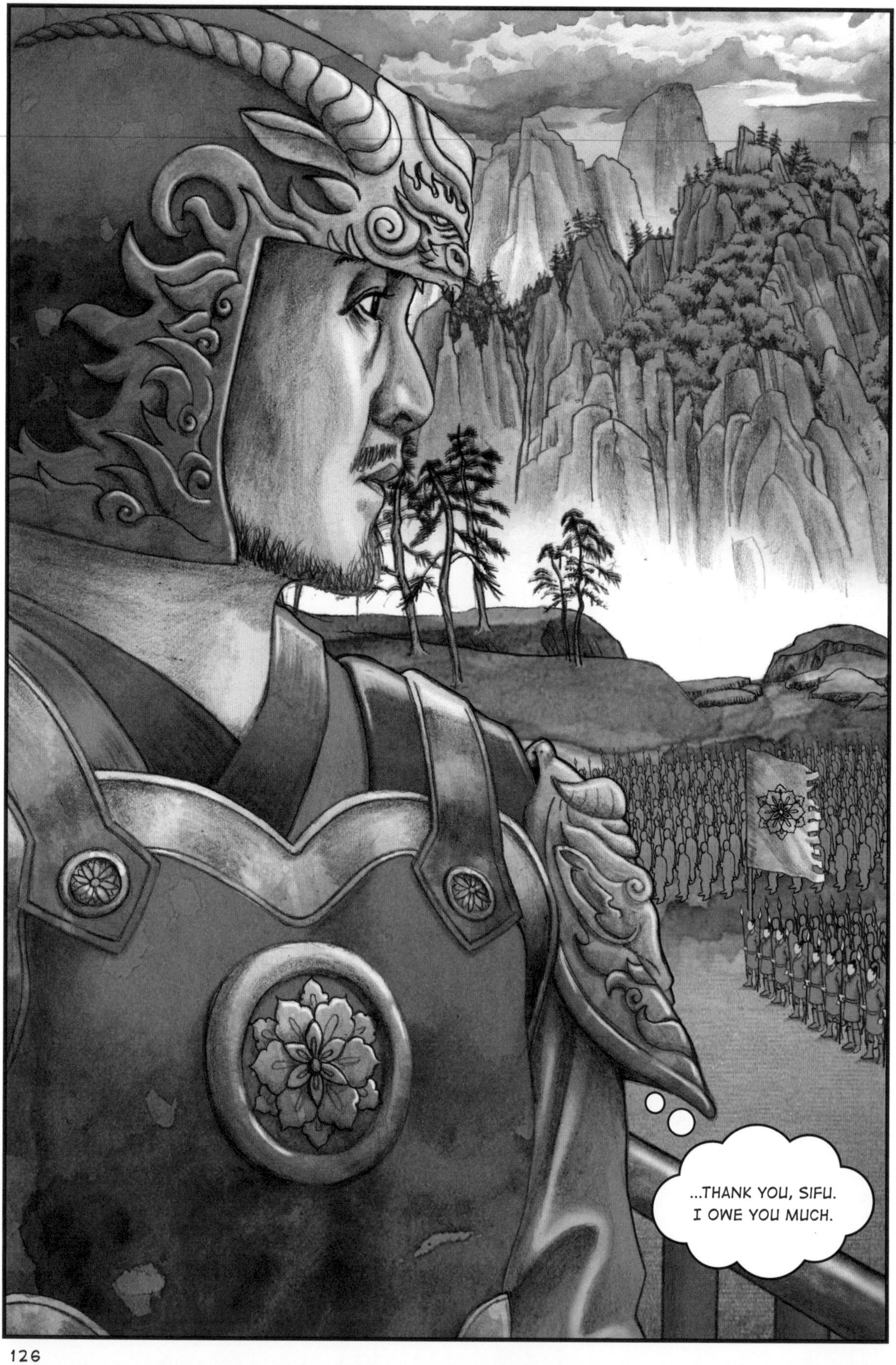
...THANK YOU, SIFU. I OWE YOU MUCH.

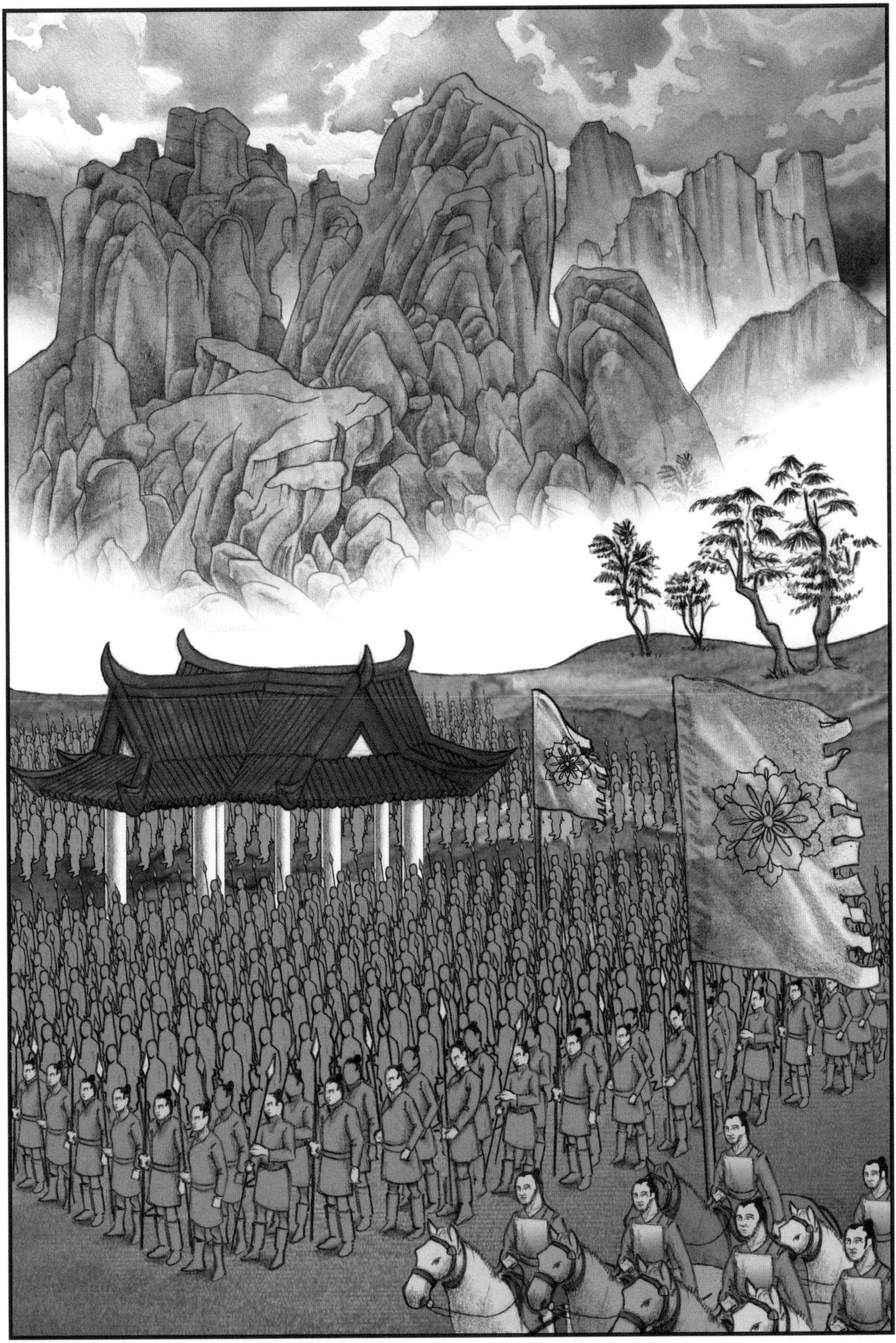

ACKNOWLEDGMENTS

Love and gratitude as always to Paul Mayor, Ma, Cos, and Ruth for their continued love and support. Big hugs to the rest of my family. Special thanks to Mike Byrne for his historical reference advice. Thanks to Lucy and James at Quarto. Thanks and big love to everyone else that puts up with me! Especially Andrew Casey, Richard Recardo, Nick Jackson, Stephen Pearce, Sebastian Cheswright Cater, Rebecca Hull, Maxine Doyle, Ben Vincent, Keith Davie, Laura Thomas, Jon King, Alex and Steph, Kevin and Francie, Han and Karolien, Alex and Ric, Simon Hayward, Bill and Vicky, Paul Ryan, Jo Lloyd, Jon Byrne, Adam and Mari, the Bad Apples, the Reckless Records crew, and all the gang from Brighton.

ABOUT THE AUTHOR AND ARTIST

Pete Katz is a half-Irish, half-Greek illustrator and gent, born in the East End of London. He has been a freelance illustrator for almost twenty years and has worked for clients including Oxfam, Barnes and Noble, *Le Monde*, Image Comics and the British Museum. He is a member of the international Bad Apple Artist Collective and produces portraits and other commissions as well as working on graphic novels. More of his work can be found at inkandmanners.com or @nutkin on Instagram.